AUSSIES in the MAJORS

Nicholas R.W. Henning

ISBN-10: 1480119792
EAN-13: 9781480119796

Contact Nicholas R.W. Henning
Email: nicholasrwhenning@hotmail.com
Blog: http://nicholasrwhenning.blogspot.com

Also by Nicholas R.W. Henning

Brennan Cooper

The American Dream: From Perth to Sacramento

The Tourist

Boomerang Baseball

CONTENTS

CHAPTER 1— THE CLEVELAND INDIANS

I was on my way to the Major Leagues, not as a player as I had once dreamed, but as the author of Australia's first baseball novel, *The American Dream: From Perth to Sacramento*, and the second, *Boomerang Baseball*.

After enjoying some sun in Honolulu from August 31, 2010, to September 5, 2010, I spent five nights in Seattle where I caught up with Lynda Lobo, a friend I made during her travel to Australia and New Zealand in 2003. My very first Major League Baseball game was thanks to Lynda, and what a game it was. The Chicago Cubs played the Pittsburgh Pirates at classic Wrigley Field on September 13, 2004. The Cubs were hunting for a playoff berth, and the atmosphere was exciting amongst 38,326 fans. The game boasted a wealth of extraordinary players; Greg Maddux was the starting pitcher for the Cubs, and he threw seven quality innings for no runs and a 7–2 victory. Maddux's career crossed three decades for a total of 355 wins and 3,371 strikeouts.

To see a Hall of Fame pitcher was amazing, yet there was quality in just about every direction I looked, with Jason Kendall catching for the Pirates and a stack of brilliant Cubs, including Aramis Ramirez, Moises Alou, Derrek Lee, and Sammy Sosa. Nomar Garciaparra was injured, but Lynda organised seats behind home plate in the company of the players' wives and guests. Garciaparra's wife, American womens' soccer great Mia Hamm, was sitting right in front of me. During that series, I asked her what she thought of Australia's womens' soccer team, the Matildas, to which see replied with an upbeat, courteous tone, "They're okay."

My 2004 trip to Chicago was a baseball bonanza as crosstown team the Chicago White Sox played at home. The highlight was on September 21, 2004, when the White Sox played the Minnesota Twins. The visiting team bullpen in right field at Cellular Field allows for fish-tank visibility from the lower level bar and dining area. I had an Aussie flag with me that I waved as some of the relief pitchers warmed up. In a flash, Australian flamethrower pitcher Grant Balfour sprinted over to the massive side window. He had made his Major League debut with the Twins on July 22, 2001, and by 2004 he was proving himself as a lights-out, late-innings pitcher. I wrote on a piece of paper, "Could we catch up after the game at the Twins' dugout?" My voice had nearly gone because of many late nights at bars on the North side of Chicago. I only drank soft drinks, yet I was reduced to a croaky mumble. Balfour nodded his head and said, "Sure, see you there!"

I was very happy, but the night got even better when Balfour came into the game and pitched an inning for no runs and one strikeout. The player he fanned was White Sox hard-hitter Paul Konerko, so during that holiday I saw one of the best pitchers in the modern era play, Greg Maddux, and an Australian participate in a Major League game. Balfour looked for me from the dugout after the game, and I waved my flag to get his attention. People watched on as he signed my Aussie flag and then fetched an official game-used Rawlings ball for me. Balfour became the second Australian to play in a World Series when he was on the Tampa Bay Rays team in 2008. It was an amazing trip, and Lynda made so much of it possible.

I only got to see Lynda for one day in Seattle, as she had to travel a few hours there and back from Olympia. After six years she was still the same, with long amber hair, a fair complexion, and ocean-blue eyes. Her car had Illinois plates and the same Cubs sticker from 2004 on the rear bumper. I had an Aussie souvenir bag full of Tim Tam biscuits (biscuits are called cookies by some Americans), Cadbury chocolate, a Southern Cross Australian T-shirt, an Aussie flag two-piece swimsuit for her, and a flag-themed beach bag. Lynda likes Australia so much that she has a kangaroo tattoo above one of her ankles.

It was ironic that we went to the bar Kangaroos and Kiwis in suburban Seattle for a long chat and a few drinks, which of course were Australian and New Zealand brands for Lynda and a soft drink for me. We talked about travel and her work in animal refuges. I have been fortunate enough to visit most regions in the world, with the exception of Africa and the Middle East, and by the end of the conversation it seemed that Lynda had reignited a desire to visit new places. It was fantastic to see her again, and she had a bag full of goodies from Olympia for me, including boutique local coffee.

My one regret in Seattle was not making an effort to see Australian pitcher Ryan Rowland-Smith, the first player in Major League Baseball history to have a hyphenated name and a solid pitcher for the Seattle Mariners. He made his debut with the Mariners on June 22, 2007, and he played with the Mariners from 2007–2010. The 2010 was a difficult season for him, and it seemed he couldn't quite get his rhythm right. He spent part of the season playing minor league baseball with the Tacoma Rainiers, and if I had been better organised, I would have known that on my second day in

Seattle the Rainiers were playing a home game. Without a car getting from Seattle to Tacoma is a long taxi ride, but it's the same suburb as the airport, so getting a cab for a decent price probably wouldn't have been that much trouble. Whenever I travel to North America, I always make sure I have a supply of packets of Tim Tams, blocks of Cadbury chocolate, and Aussie flag paraphernalia attire. I'm sure Rowland-Smith would have appreciated some Aussie flag board shorts, as he is an avid surfer, and some Tim Tams and Cadbury chocolate might have made his day.

From Seattle Tacoma International Airport, I flew on Continental Airlines CO274, at 7:25 a.m., on Friday, September 10, 2010, to Hopkins International Airport in Cleveland, Ohio, arriving at 2:45 p.m. My entire visual knowledge of Cleveland had been cultivated based on what I had seen during television coverage of Indians games during the 1990s, the film *Major League* and the sitcom *The Drew Carey Show*. Key Tower, the BP Building, and the Terminal Tower defined the skyline of the Cleveland I knew. These structures are the tallest in the city and represent different periods of architecture. The Terminal Tower had become my favourite, though, with an American flag always sailing from its highest point and all the elegance of an early twentieth century building with stonework crafted by skilful masons.

It was a clear afternoon as I made my way to the airport taxi rank, wheeling two cricket kit bags, which was my entire luggage. One had all my clothes and travel needs and the other full of Aussie paraphernalia to give away during my trip. I hoped to fill this bag with souvenirs as it gradually emptied. I was allocated a taxi based on a numbered ticket system, which was monitored by an attendant to ensure all the drivers got a fair piece of the patronage. "Can I help you with those, sir?" my taxi driver asked as he unhesitatingly picked up my bags and loaded them in the boot. "So where to?"

"The Holiday Inn Express on Euclid Avenue, please."

"You're Australian?" he queried with an enthusiastic tone.

"Yes, I'm from Sydney," I replied, feeling pleased he recognized my accent so easily.

"I really want to visit there." I would soon learn this was a frequent sentiment among many of the Americans I met along the way. It was nice to know that Australia seemed to be such a popular tourist destination for Americans. As we drove, our conversation flowed easily, "So are you a ballplayer with all that gear?" It was tempting to say yes and no doubt enjoy his undivided attention and probably sign an autograph for him once I reached my destination.

"I used to play in Australia, but I'm here because I wrote two Aussie baseball-themed novels, and I'm visiting a friend who works in the front office of the Cleveland Indians."

"That's real neat. I think we've had one Aussie play with the Indians. I can't remember his name, though."

I knew instantly who it was. "Yes, Cameron Cairncross played for the Indians during the year 2000."

"Sure, that's him; he looked okay, but he got hurt."

"It was a shame because he had worked hard for the opportunity at a time when the Indians were in a bit of a golden era," I added. The Indians had certainly proved their commitment to Australian talent; all through the 2000s, they signed young Aussie prospects in good numbers. Cairncross debuted on July 20, 2000, and played his last game on October 1, 2000. His ERA was 3.86 over 9.1 innings pitched with eight strikeouts.

"Are there Aussies within the Indians farm system right now?" he asked.

"Yes, a few who are quite notable too. Relief pitcher Shane Lindsay was selected off waivers from the New York Yankees on June 1, 2010, and he's playing some AA and AAA. The other is an outfielder named Jason Smit. He signed for apparently close to half a million dollars when no Aussie has signed for that kind of money in a long time. He's playing at A-ball level at the moment, but he's a gifted player who has Major League tools."

"You sure know plenty about baseball!"

The future was bright for Lindsay. He signed with the Chicago White Sox in 2011 and made his Major League debut on September 2, 2011. Jason Smit walked away from baseball in 2011. He spent 2007–2011 within the Indians farm system, and at twenty-one years old decided a professional baseball career wasn't for him anymore. I nearly fell off my chair when I read news of his decision. He had spent most of the years between ages seventeen and twenty-one half a world away from his family and friends in Perth, Western Australia and that no doubt contributed to the decline in his desire to play.

My taxi driver said he would check out my books on Amazon when he finished his shift and there I was on Euclid Avenue within walking distance to Progressive Field, home of the Cleveland Indians. I unpacked some of my luggage and took a shower. There was still some office hours left in the day, so I rang Marlene Lehky, executive assistant to the Indians President and General Manager Mark Shapiro. I've known Marlene since 2009. She had kindly responded to communication from me that year regarding my book *The American Dream: From Perth to Sacramento* and was among the first to read a copy. We stayed in contact and I discovered we shared an interest in travel and seeing new places, and Australia was a destination she hoped to visit one day. Marlene was a thoughtful person, and when the 2009 dust storm swept over Sydney on September 23, 2009, making the whole city look like the planet Mars, she e-mailed me to make sure I was okay. At last I had an opportunity to meet her.

With a bag full of packets of Tim Tams, I walked up to the Indians' front office entrance. A nice man at the reception asked me who I wanted to see and requested that I sign in.

"I have a Nicholas Henning from Australia to see you Marlene," he said into a phone. He put down the handset and told me Marlene would be a few moments. I was slightly nervous as I was meeting her for the first time. A door opened, and with a friendly smile Marlene walked toward me and said, "Hello, Nick, welcome to Cleveland." Her warm nature matched her convivial tone. Thanks to Marlene, I was a guest of a baseball club which is an international brand. I remember from 1994 to 1997, watching ESPN baseball games featuring the Indians, late at night, and marvelling at what was then known as Jacobs Field and the super teams they had in the 1990s. Jim Thome and Kenny Loften were my favourite two players from that special era. Renamed Progressive Field, it was like a cathedral to me, and to be there was a dream come true.

For Australians, the idea of a centralised playing venue and front office isn't so familiar, as many sporting teams in Australia rent a playing facility and even the sports clubs which own their grounds usually have an office well away from the field. The centralisation common in North American sports is a logistical advantage, and eventually more sports in Australia will probably take the same direction.

"I'd like to introduce you to Mark, but he's out of town."

Mark Shapiro was well known to Indians fans, but film and baseball enthusiasts across the world later came to know him from the 2011 movie *Moneyball.* In it there was a scene involving Mark, played by Reed Diamond, and the Oakland Athletics General Manager Billy Beane, played by Brad Pitt, discussing player trades. The scene in the film, with them talking face to face and various Indians associates in the meeting was fictionalised, as general managers usually don't negotiate in person—yet it was an enjoyable scene which helped compress a complicated process. Marlene explained the Hollywood adaptation of events in an e-mail to me in December 2011. It would have been great to meet Mark when I was in Cleveland, but I had a few packets of Tim Tams for him, which Marlene passed on, to let him know I was there and very grateful to be a guest of the Indians.

Australian-made Tim Tams are so popular in the US that Australia should brand them as a national biscuit. Vegemite has never taken off in the US, but Tim Tams could go a long way there. There are American-made Tim Tams, but they're not the same as slightly different ingredients are used, which alters the taste.

Marlene showed me around the front office, and it was fantastic to see where so many important decisions are made regarding the club. The walls were decorated with photographs of past Indians' teams, players, and great moments from the club's history. Then it happened: sixteen-years in the making, standing in an executive suite, I got to see Progressive Field with my own eyes for the first time. The batting practice cage was on the field as game time was still a few hours away, at 7:05 p.m. The three white toothbrush lights standing above the scoreboard in left field and the Indians neon sign in red with gold-yellow outlining the scoreboard brought back memories of me as a fifteen-year old baseball fanatic. Even back then I never imagined I would actually be in Cleveland, the outfield grass was immaculate with diagonal mowing lines and the infield dirt looked like it had been sculpted with engineering precision. The infield grass would have made any green keeper at a golf course proud. I knew I was very fortunate to be there. All my Christmases had come at once; the Minnesota Twins were visiting and I had tickets to all the games. Not just any tickets! I had scout tickets sitting behind home plate in section 154, row R, seat number 1.

Even though I'd be throwing my support behind the Indians, the Twins have a deep connection to Australian baseball. Historically, the Twins have signed more Aussies to professional contracts than any other club. By the conclusion of the 2010 season, six Australians had played Major League Baseball with the Twins, which at the time was the highest number of Aussies to have played for one club at that level. On April 28, 2010, West Australian Luke Hughes made his debut with the Twins and hit a home run in his first at-bat! But he spent most of the 2010 season on the disabled list and any hope of seeing him play in Cleveland was dashed by a season-ending injury. Yet my Aussie fix had been satisfied well before I arrived in Cleveland with the Los Angeles Angels of Anaheim visiting the Indians on September 14 and Australian relief pitcher Richard Thompson was on their roster.

The Twins were leading the American League Central Division and the Indians were well out of the playoff race, yet the Indians played like a team that hadn't given up. On Friday September 10, the Indians beat the Twins 2–0. Fausto Carmona dominated; pitching all nine innings for the Indians, striking out seven, and only giving up three hits. All 26,207 baseball fans got to witness a pitching clinic that night. On Saturday, September 11, the game went into extra innings before Jim Thome sealed the win with a solo home run in the twelfth inning. It was a hard-fought game, with the Twins winning 1–0. The crowd of 24,972 didn't know whether to clap or throw their popcorn on the ground after seeing an Indians favourite whack the ball deep over the fence in a Twins uniform. I was pleased to see him hit a home run with my own eyes. The Twins raced away with the game on Sunday, September 12, scoring five runs in the first inning and eventually winning 6–2. The 22,988 in attendance could only wonder if it wasn't for that tearaway first inning, perhaps it may have been a win for the Indians.

Watching a Major League Baseball game in the US is seeing the sport played in its most pure form. The smoothness of infield plays is choreographed with precision. The big hitting is thunderous and the speed and accuracy of pitching shows the dual skills of the hitter and pitcher going head to head like matador and a bull. The batter is the bull who is expected to fail seven out of ten times. In Australia, seeing a pitcher hit low nineties miles per hour in velocity is considered very decent pace, however during that Twins and Indians series I was seeing 95 mph to 98 mph flash up on the radar readings consistently, I thought, "Wow, that's around 158 kilometres per hour, and they are pitching at that speed deep into the game too." I find it pleasing to see the patriotism which comes with baseball in the US, as an American flag is often stitched onto the players' uniforms and there are always multiple flags sailing around the field.

During the Twins series I had the same hot dog vendor servicing the area I was sitting in. Dragging out the first letter of each word, he shouted, "Hhot ddogs! Hhot ddogs!" It looked like hard work as he had to carry a steel vending box which kept the food warm, and he was continually walking up and down the aisles in sections behind home plate and as far left as third base and as far right as first base. He wore a uniform which included a red and white striped shirt. I admired his effort and purchased two to three hotdogs per game. By the second innings he had sweat running down his face. I gave him a few dollars tip each night. It was an authentic baseball experience watching the game and munching on a hotdog. The Indians hotdogs are more compact than those in Australia. They are tightly packed in a bun no bigger than my hand, where back home the frankfurts are long and daggle out each end of a slightly longer bun. The Indians' hotdogs came in plenty of varieties, including additions uncommon in Australia, like chilli topping. The Aussie hotdog frankfurts are a bit tasteless compared to those from America; I found they had a richer, stronger taste with a bit more smokiness to them.

For the last inning of the game, I stood under the left centre field bleacher stand on September 12 as John Adams, the Indians bass drummer, beat out a "boom, boom, boom!" Since August 24, 1973, he had only missed thirty-four games, which showed very impressive dedication to the club. During the 1995 World Series, I remember the television cameras zooming in on him a few times. Being there was one of many moments when I had to pinch myself to believe I was really experiencing it all.

I had told Marlene before I arrived in the US, Richard Thompson was on the roster for the visiting Angels and it would be great to somehow have a chance to talk with him during my visit. September 15, 2010, is a special day amongst all my greatest baseball experiences. Marlene organised an Indians press credential for me which allowed me to set foot on the field whilst the players were completing their warm up. When she handed me the credential, she said with a warm smile, "Now you go and catch up with your friend." My brain was spinning at the thought of walking on the field and rubbing shoulders with Major League Baseball players. "Marlene, thank you very much. This is the most amazing opportunity I have ever had." Her kindness and generosity made a list of dreams come true during my visit. In my calendar of important dates to remember, I declared going forward September 15 to be Marlene Lehky Day.

As I strolled onto Progressive Field, I felt engulfed in euphoria. I had a bag with three pairs of Aussie board shorts to hand out—one for Richard and I hadn't decided on whom else would be a recipient, but planned to give them all out as I had three pairs still left for my next stop in Kansas City. It was changeover from the Indians batting practice to the Angels. I suddenly realised if I wanted to talk to any Indians players, I needed to be quick about it because they'd all be off the field quite soon. South Korean outfielder and talented hitter Shin-Soo Choo was standing looking out at the field. "Hello, mate, how's your day going?" I asked cheerfully. He didn't even take a second to blink and replied, "You're Australian?"

"Yep, sure am."

Choo has a decent command of English and asked me with a spark of excitement, "Do you know Craig Anderson, Chris Snelling, and Travis Blackley? I played with them when I was with Seattle." During the late 1990s and early 2000s, several Australians signed with the Seattle Mariners. I followed all their careers closely; outfielder Snelling made his Major League debut with the Mariners on May 25, 2002, and pitcher Travis Blackley on July 1, 2004. Craig Anderson, also a pitcher, made it to AAA with both the Mariners and Orioles. He was unlucky not to get a shot at the Majors with the

Orioles despite a 7–3 win/loss record and a 2.98 ERA at AAA level during the 2007 season.

I replied to Choo, "I know who they all are; they've done a lot for baseball on behalf of Australia. I have something I would like to give you." Choo looked at me curiously as I reached into my carry bag and handed him a pair of Aussie flag board shorts.

"Very nice. Are they for snowboarding?"

I actually think he meant surfboarding not snowboarding, but I clarified for him anyway. "No, they are shorts you wear when you go to the beach and surf or swim." He examined them, carefully running his fingers over the stitching. "Thank you. The colours are like those of South Korea." He shook my hand and smiled. As he walked into the Cleveland dugout and made his way along the player tunnel to the clubhouse, it felt good knowing I'd given a player who had .300 or higher batting average from 2008–2010 something uniquely Australian.

As of the 2010 Major League Baseball season, three Australians had played at that level with the Angels. Australia's first Major Leaguer of the modern baseball era, infielder Craig Shipley, wore the Angels uniform before any other Aussie. He played there for one season in 1998, and his final game was on September 25, 1998. Trent Durrington was the first Australian to debut with the Angels, achieving this on August 6, 1999. He played Majors with the Angels for portions of seasons from 1999–2003. Relief pitcher Richard Thompson has proven himself the most enduring. He made his Major League debut on September 1, 2007 and spent parts of each season from 2007–2010 as a Major Leaguer. The year 2010 was his breakthrough season; he achieved two wins and no losses and his ERA was 1.37 over 19.2 innings pitched, with fifteen strikeouts. Thompson and I grew up in the same area of Sydney on the Upper North Shore; he was born in Hornsby and I was born in Wahroonga. We both went to schools in the local area and lived within a few suburbs of each other. Even though he is a few years younger than me, I'm sure we both stood on Hornsby Train Station on our way to school plenty of times. I recall occasions during the 2004–2005 Sydney Major League season sitting in the opposite dugout from him, when he played with the Ryde Hawks and I played for North Shore. But despite just a few metres between us, we didn't meet during that season.

I was worried he may not come out in time for me to see him. I asked some Japanese journalists who were reporting on Angels' Japanese slugger Hideki "Godzilla" Matsui's every move if they could see if Richard was in the clubhouse and to ask for him, which they kindly did. I had learnt some Japanese in high school, and the fact that I could say a few greeting introductions, some basic sentences and to express gratitude brought a smile to the journalists' faces even though their English was excellent. A few minutes later, he came out of the visitors' dugout and noticed that I was wearing a grey Macquarie University sweatshirt, which is our local university. I waved and smiled at him. He put out his hand and we shook. His firm grip made me appreciate the thousands of times he'd probably gripped a baseball or spent hours training. "How's it going?" He seemed surprised half a world away from Australia, to be talking with an Aussie on Progressive Field. He asked, "What's your name and what brings you here?"

"My name's Nick Henning. I'm here as a guest of the Indians, and I'm also trying to promote my two Aussie-themed baseball books." As he seemed interested I said, "There's plenty you'll know in my book *Boomerang Baseball.* It's a bit of a local Sydney baseball story somewhat based on me." Uncertain how long I'd have to talk with him I got straight to the point. "I have something for you." I rustled out a pair of Aussie flag board shorts from my bag. "I hope the size is right, but you know, something from home."

"Thank you." He said with an appreciative grin. "I live over here these days, and a reminder of home is good. I try and get back for a few weeks each year."

"If you've got a teammate who has a bit of a big backside, I have another pair in my bag which are roomy and…" I was just about to finish my sentence when I heard an American accent swoop in from the side, "I can help you with that and I'm from Florida."

I looked at Richard, who said, "Nick, this is Bobby Wilson." We shook hands. Wilson was the Angels' bench catcher and quite handy with the bat too. "Okay, good. I want to get a photograph of the two of you holding up your Aussie board shorts," and then Wilson took a snap of Richard and I together. "Where are you going after here?" Richard asked.

"I'm heading down to Kansas City to see the Royals play the Indians, my invitation is from the Royals."

"Can you do a favour for me?"

"Sure."

"There's a friend of ours playing for the Royals, a pitcher, Sean O'Sullivan. We played together for a few years, and he's from San Diego. If you've got any more Aussie stuff to give out, he'd love something."

"I have three pairs of Aussie flag board shorts left."

"Great, he's a bit of a surfer." Richard and Bobby Wilson had to leave a few moments later as they had to help out with batting practice, taking balls in the outfield and at some stage Wilson would probably need to take some swings.

That night, Angels ace pitcher Jered Weaver threw seven innings for just one hit, struck out seven, and took the win in a game that ended 7–0. I wasn't there to see it, but the Indians bounced back on September 16 to win 3–2.

My time in Cleveland allowed me to tick many boxes on my baseball wish list, all thanks to Marlene Lehky. When I returned to Australia, I sent her a box full of Tim Tams and Cadbury chocolate. We exchanged a few e-mails between November 9–16. She wrote:

> Everyone here is loving the Cadbury and Tim Tam biscuits. I took some home for Bill and will take one of each to my parents. They are both eighty-five years of age and love sweets! Of course, I am keeping a supply for myself…Thank you again for your generosity…The candy and Tim Tams continue to be a hit. I took some to my parents over the weekend and they proclaimed that the biscuits are the best they have ever had! Thanks again

It's nice to know several people enjoyed some Australian treats, and each year on Marlene Lehky Day I try to send a box of Tim Tams and Cadbury chocolate to her. I have discovered her favourites from the Tim Tam varieties are original flavour and the double coated.

My baseball jet-setting had another great stop ahead of me in Kansas City; I had plenty of Aussie paraphernalia to hand out and another amazing baseball experience waiting for me.

CHAPTER 2
THE KANSAS CITY ROYALS

On September 16, 2010, it was a rainy morning, which delayed my flight to Kansas City Missouri. Continental CO2426 departed about an hour later than planned yet I wasn't bothered as it was only a two-hour flight from Cleveland. I arrived at Kansas City International Airport at around 11:00 a.m. and the airport terminal was quite compact with no long labyrinth of passageways to walk through. It seemed only a short walk through the terminal to the security area. I assumed the thick wall of glass was a partition, but it was actually the only divide between arriving and departing passengers. I was surprised when I cleared security after just a short line. If only more travel was so easy. When a door amongst the glass barrier slid open for me, I liked the airport even more as it was a smooth process and within minutes I was on my way.

I took a taxi from the airport to the Holiday Inn Express Kansas City—Westport Plaza. The driver wasn't chatty but I didn't mind, as I wanted to stare out the window and take it all in. I also asked to be driven through the city, rather than the most direct route to my hotel. I imagined Kansas City and Missouri to be dry, yet the steady flow of grassy agricultural land, parks, and gardens skirting the road from the airport and especially around the city, made me realise all the old Kansas City Westerns I had watched as a kid were probably shot somewhere else. The cityscape had a noticeable row of about ten or twelve high-rise buildings. Apart from this concentrated area, the city was gently spread out with many other edifices under ten storeys high. One building which stood out for me was the world headquarters for H&R Block, with its modern and trendy design. Usually buildings associated with taxation aren't known for their beauty. Completed in 2006, it is eighteen-storeys high and oval shaped with shiny, big glass windows from top to bottom, chromed metal fixtures around the base and lower levels. The main glass exterior has a soft green colour to it, with an easy street address to remember! 1 H&R Block Way, Kansas City. I like how they do that in America, and sport is no exception with the Royals Kauffman Stadium address as 1 Royal Way Kansas City.

I'd known Don Free since 2009. Like Marlene, he had kindly responded to communication regarding my book *The American Dream: From Perth to Sacramento*. Don is the manager of operations for the Royals Radio Network, with the key responsibility as producer/engineer of the Royals radio coverage, which is one of the largest broadcast areas in Major League Baseball, going as far north as South Dakota and down to Oklahoma and Arkansas. I was completely knocked off my feet when Don told me Royals Radio announcer Steve Stewart wanted to interview me in his pregame show on July 3, 2009. It was my first-ever radio interview and the first time I appeared in any form of American media.

Fresh on Stewart's mind was Melbourne-born slugger Justin Huber, the likeable Aussie Royals player who took to the diamond as an outfielder, first baseman, and designated hitter with stints from 2005–2007. He also played with the San Diego Padres in 2008 and Minnesota Twins in 2009. Huber was the first Australian to debut in the Major Leagues with the Royals achieving this on June 21, 2005. I could feel Stewart's smile through the phone when he mentioned Huber, who is known for his warm and larrikin personality. Don spoke well of Huber too and was pleased to have met him during his time at the Royals.

As of 2010, two Aussies were on the Royals playing alumni. The first was Graeme Lloyd, who spent part of the 2003 season there and he played his final game as a Major Leaguer with the Royals on September 27, 2003. Graeme Lloyd is one of my favourite Australian baseball players of all time, along with Brendan Kingman. Lloyd was the first Aussie to attain a Baseball World Series ring, and has two as a member of the 1996 and 1998 New York Yankees. One of the true gentlemen of Australian baseball, he was the first Major Leaguer I ever met, in early 1994, on Queensland's Gold Coast where the then East Coast Cougars played the Perth Heat and he was on the Heat team. The Royals connection to Australia is deeper than just Major Leaguers, as the Kansas City Royals in the fifth round of the 1993 Major League Baseball June amateur draft drafted Canberra-born pitcher Phil Brassington. Brassington played low A ball within the Royals farm system in 1993 with a 2.42 ERA and pitching 48.1 innings. Unfortunately, injury stopped Brassington's promising professional career, but not to be beaten he reinvented himself as a nasty junk ball pitcher and played independent baseball in the US from 1999–2003. He also played for Australia at various international tournaments and pitched on the inaugural 2010/2011 Canberra Cavalry team of the new Australian Baseball League. At forty years old, he looked at least five years younger than his actual age, and pitched plenty of filthy junk balls which bamboozled batters.

My interview with Steve Stewart was a big break for me. Our discussion focused on the Aussies who had played for

Kansas City, Royals legend George Brett who worked with the Australian team during the 2009 World Baseball Classic and of course my book. It was an amazing experience. Thanks to Don and Steve I had made it to American airwaves.

You only have to look at Don to know he's a good guy. He has an earnest smile which sometimes sits under a snowy moustache and his grin shows the top row of his teeth with a small gap between the two top front teeth. His sky blue eyes reflect a gentle soul, shining behind metal-framed spectacles and his face looks naturally accustomed to contentment with an easy upward tilt to both sides of his face. The Royals feature short biographies and a photograph of their broadcasters so I knew what Don looked like long before I met him.

Many sports announcers/commentators in the US are career broadcasters, who have spent years refining their skills. Whilst former players also contribute to the calling of games, it seems the professional commentators represent the majority. In Australian sports, it is former players who appear to be the higher proportion of commentators, particularly with televised games. The downside of this is the former players don't always have the voice or training to be an engaging broadcaster, yet they have expert knowledge of the game, so they are informative, but nothing beats a lucid, strong voice calling a game.

Royals Radio Announcer Steve Stewart had been broadcasting sports since he was a student at Southern Methodist University and called baseball games on radio and television for over twenty years. His voice was clear and commanding, and he was a neat, presentable fellow. When I heard his voice for the first time, on the telephone, back in July 2009, I thought to myself he could add value in Australia as a broadcaster of baseball or basketball. North American accents in

Australian sports leagues too often belong to former players and to have a career American commentator call sports in Australia would add extra spark. If the Australian Baseball League picked up a season television deal in the future, someone like Steve could add some real shine. I regret not telling Steve this when I spoke with him in 2009, I had the opportunity to do so when I visited in 2010, but there was so much going on that I didn't want to distract him from his work preparing for or undertaking his broadcast.

After over a year of intermittent contact, the opportunity to meet Don and Steve arrived on September 17, 2010. Don collected me from my hotel and it was astounding to think that the distance of half a world away was gone and we were standing in person at last. I had told him I would bring some Aussie attire and goodies, which included Tim Tams. As a sports enthusiast, the most appropriate garment for Don was an easy choice. I had for him an official Wallabies Rugby Union jersey with its bright gold-yellow colour, the Australian Rugby Union crest on the left side of the upper chest, a wallaby on the right and a Qantas Airways sponsorship tag across the lower chest. Unknown to me until I met him, Don has the build of a retired rugby union prop with a broad sturdiness.

I wondered if Don would be asked by people where the jersey was from when he wore it, and it crossed my mind he might be mistaken for an Aussie in the company of local rugby union pundits and ones from overseas. I was taken by surprise to find rugby union has a reasonable following in the US and stumbled across plenty of Americans during my travels who follow the game. Rugby is played at various US colleges and receives television coverage in some areas. If a professional competition were to be established in the US, they could develop into a competitive outfit given their population and sports-crazy culture. Don appreciated the gifts and we drove off to Kauffman Stadium.

On the way to the stadium we stopped for some famous Kansas City smoky flame-grilled beef and pork ribs. The restaurant was local, not a franchise of any kind, and I was so hungry I didn't even take the time to notice the name of the place. When my ribs and beef were delivered to our table I tried not to eat like a barbarian, but probably did, having missed breakfast.

I checked an eating guide at the hotel whilst waiting for Don and it made me laugh. Fosters Beer and Outback Steakhouse had a small write-up, yet back in Australia both are well behind other local market leaders. In America, each is promoted with the 1980s Paul Hogan larrikin-style of humour, portraying Australia with rural or beach lifestyle and those famous words "shrimp on the barbie, mate!" For those Americans who venture to Australia and arrive in Sydney or Melbourne the advertising of Australia is quite different to how most people live and of course the language used in normal conversation. Each city has a population of over five million people.

As we made our way to the stadium, Don said with great enthusiasm, "Australia is on the bucket list! It's one place overseas I dream of visiting." Just like in Cleveland, the fascination with Australia from Americans pleased me. "But it's an expensive flight down there, right?"

I replied, "It is a bit pricey, but food and accommodation are a lot cheaper than places in Europe like France and England."

Truman Sports Complex, which consists of Arrowhead and Kauffman Stadium, rises like two big castles. Arrowhead is where gridiron is played and home of the Kansas City Chiefs. Just like in Cleveland, my only knowledge of

Kauffman Stadium was what I had seen from baseball telecasts. I remember during the mid-1990s, the playing surface switching from Astroturf to grass, but a lot I was seeing for the first time. Taking the front office entrance and then the lift up to the broadcast booth made me realise yet again I was one lucky Aussie! I had my team-coloured blue and white press credential around my neck, which permitted me access to everywhere except the clubhouse.

Don was the first of the radio team to arrive. The radio broadcast booth was like a seat in heaven with a perfect view of the whole field, probably two to three storeys above the field. I suddenly realised lots of people would pay thousands of dollars to be sitting where I was and my books had taken me to this very sacred vantage point to watch and experience Major League Baseball.

Steve Stewart was next to arrive and when Don introduced me to him he said with warm enthusiasm, "Welcome to Kansas City, it's great to finally meet you." We shook hands, and I gave him an Australian Cricket Team polo shirt. He unfolded the shirt, briefly examining it and then his face became quite serious, "Thank you so much for thinking of me, Nick."

It seemed to be that time of day as more announcers arrived, which included the television announcers, who were situated in the broadcast booth next to us. I instantly recognised Jeff Montgomery. I had plenty of baseball cards of him. In the 1980s and early 1990s he was featured with hair close to shoulder length. His hairstyle had changed to short and tidy and he didn't look like a forty-eight-year old man. He wasn't bald or greying, and head to toe he still had a slenderness about him suggesting an active life. Montgomery was a lights-out, late innings pitcher who played for the Royals from 1988–1999, and his final Major League game was in a

Royals uniform, on October 2, 1999. When Don introduced me to him it seemed like the perfect opportunity to open up a pack of Tim Tams for everyone to enjoy. "These have come all the way from Australia," I said proudly.

"Hmm, nice," was the chorus from Don, Jeff, and Steve after eating one. Jeff asked me what brought me to Kansas City and I told him about my books. I added, "You made the news in Australia back in 1991."

"Really? For baseball?"

"Yes, but the story was more about professional sport, which included NBA basketball and at the time Australian sports weren't yet fully professional. News of your contract for that year and many others made people wonder if athletes across all major sports in Australia might one day be full-time and be able to earn a similar income." Montgomery's salary for 1991 was $1,065,000.

"I didn't know that. That's interesting."

"You look fit enough to be still playing."

Montgomery gave a humble laugh and replied, "About ten years ago I was." It was surreal to be in the company of a person who was a Major League Baseball All-Star in 1992, 1993, and 1996, a period of time when baseball was the centre of my universe.

There are multiple levels to the front office and media areas and Don took me to meet some other staff. He introduced me to Dina Wathan, coordinator for media services and mentioned I was visiting from Australia. Tall, beautiful, and down to earth, Dina took me by surprise when she asked me, "Do you know Jason Horne?"

"Yes, I know him. He purchased a copy of my first baseball book last year and we've been in contact by e-mail since. He seems like a good guy."

"Yeah, he's nice and he's been part of fantasy camp here." I met Jason later that year at a baseball game in Australia. It was easy to spot him as he had a Royals jersey on, with his surname and the number 1 on the back and wearing a Royals cap. Dina added, "Justin Huber used to play here a few years ago." It was pleasing Huber had made such an impact at so many levels of the club during his time with the Royals.

"He spent this year in Japan. I'm hoping he plays in the new Australian Baseball League, as I've never seen him play on home soil and our league plays during your winter, which is summer time for us."

Don and I took the lift down to field level and we walked through the underbelly of the stadium, where to my surprise there are hitting cages and just a few steps away the Royals players' dugout. It was so much to take in at once as Royals players walked around me and the place where all the magic happened, the field, was lit with sunshine despite some clouds drifting across the blue sky. Steve Stewart had made his way down to the field and was close by, organising some interview material for the pregame radio show. A Royals print journalist was talking with Don. Right in front of me stood Billy Butler with a bat in his hand, having taken a break from some batting practice. Butler, a first baseman or designated hitter for the Royals, proved his skills as a Major League hitter by finishing second in the American League in doubles hit during the 2009 season and fourth in doubles by the end of the 2010 season. He consistently hit around .300 and gave plenty of pop to the Royals batting line up.

I have learnt the opportunity to talk often only comes once, so I took the chance while I had it. I didn't want him to think I was going to hassle him with a lot of chat so I kept it brief and started walking toward the dugout entrance and turned and looked at him, “Billy, it’s good to see you.” I wish I could have come up with something better than that, but in a split second that’s what came out of my mouth. He looked at me a little confused, probably a combination of not having seen me before and wondering where my accent was from. I smiled and walked into the dugout.

There was a very familiar face among the coaching staff. Kevin Seitzer started his career as a Royal and played in blue and white from 1986–1991. He then had some stints with the Milwaukee Brewers, from 1992–1996, and played with some other clubs. Despite his reliable hitting and good work playing mostly infield positions, it was his signature flattop hairstyle which came to mind when I saw him. I wondered if under his baseball cap his crew cut was still the same. He had been featured in an early 1990s British documentary on Bo Jackson, an all-star in both baseball and gridiron, as they were teammates at the Royals. It was a good opportunity to chat with him a little, because the Royals were wrapping up their batting practice on the field, which he was overseeing. A few minutes later, batting was finished and he grabbed a drink. I walked closer to him, and while he took a moment to relax I said, “Hello, Kevin, it’s great to see you coaching here.”

“Thanks. Are you Australian?” I never get sick of that question in America because it always leads to something which makes me feel proud to be an Aussie. “Yes, I’m from Sydney.”

“Do you know Dave Nilsson and Graeme Lloyd? I played with them at the Brewers.” I suddenly realised Seitzer had been witness to the rise of two of Australia’s best baseball players, as his time there perfectly coincided with theirs. “I followed their careers quite closely and they are both still involved in baseball in Australia.”

"Good. There was another guy on the Brewers team, he's American but spent plenty of time down there, John Jaha."

"Oh yes, J.J. played for the Daikyo Dolphins on the Queensland Gold Coast, in the former Australian Baseball League. I think he played two seasons for them during the early 1990s. That guy was a hit machine!"

"So what brings you here?"

"I'm a guest of the Royals Radio Network. I have written a couple of Aussie-themed baseball books. Have you still got that famous flattop?" He smiled and lifted his cap, revealing rows of spiky hair. It was nice after all those years he was very much the Kevin I remembered. I added, "The last I heard you were in a partnership running a baseball school?"

He said "It's real busy there at the moment and I also have commitments here." I had a feeling that at any minute he would need to take off and work with some of the hitters in the batting cages.

"Kevin, it's great to see you, and I'm pleased that you're sharing your hitting expertise with this club." We shook hands, and he walked over toward the batting cages.

With hardly anyone around, I took the opportunity to do what I had always dreamed of and sat in a Major League Baseball dugout. I rode the pine, as they say and for a few minutes I enjoyed the view of the job I had wanted so much as an adolescent. Don told me I could stay down at the field until the various practice sessions had finished, but he needed to return to the radio broadcast booth to complete further preparations. I took the opportunity to walk through the stadium underbelly toward the visiting Indians dugout. Walking the other way back to the Royals dugout was Sean O'Sullivan, the pitcher who was friends with Richard Thompson and Bobby Wilson from the Angels. I had goodies in a plastic bag with me, and I wasn't going to let the opportunity slip.

"Hello, Sean."

He stopped and gave me his full attention and I had to look up to this tall fellow, who has the build of a rugby union second rower. In baseball terms, his build was more like a slugger than a pitcher. I continued talking, "I was just in Cleveland and saw some of the Angels series. Your mates Bobby Wilson and Richard Thompson send their regards, but I've been told to look after you with some Aussie paraphernalia." I rustled through the bag and pulled out a pair of Aussie flag board shorts for him. It wasn't often I expected to make a stranger's day, especially a Major League Baseball player, yet a big smile beamed across O'Sullivan's face. "Thank you. I really appreciate it. I surf back home."

"I hope the size is okay, they might be a little tight."

"They should do fine, thank you again." He shook my hand and his grip was like an Olympic weight lifter's strength. Knowing I might be pressed for time, I headed back to the Royals dugout with two pairs of shorts left to give out.

There were plenty of players scattered about the dugout area and for a moment I was stuck wondering who I would give them to. Walking in catcher's leggings with his glove in hand was Brayan Pena, but that's not what caught my attention. A friendly smile was constant on his face, which conveyed a cheerful guy enjoying his work. He wasn't even looking in my direction, yet all the indicators suggested walking over to him and giving him a pair of Aussie flag board shorts would be fine. "Hello, Brayan, how are you today?" I had his attention and his smile stretched even further across his face. "Where are you from?" he asked me in his Latino-accented English.

"I'm from Australia."

A wave of energy came over him, to suggest I had solved a small mystery for him and his eyes widened. "Ah, okay great. Aussie! Aussie! Oi! Oi!" He raised his arm and fist as he said Australia's national sporting war cry. "I'm Cuban and I've played against Australian teams."

I was taken aback and very pleased with his warm enthusiasm. "I have something for you from Australia." I said as I retrieved a pair of board shorts and handed them to him.

He unfolded them and his smile just kept growing. "Ah. Thank you. I live in Florida." He shook my hand and wished me well. I knew it had been a good idea to hand out Aussie-themed clothing. Out of all the players it was Pena who had taken me by surprise.

With just one pair left, I had noticed a rookie outfielder doing some sprint work a bit earlier. This young fellow had speed which could leave any rugby union quick outside back chasing in his tracks. Kevin Seitzer walked past, and I pointed to the player and asked Kevin his name, "Jarrod Dyson." I waited for Dyson to stop in the dugout as he gathered some of his bats.

"Hello," I said. He took a moment to think, perhaps trying to determine if he recognised me. "I have something for you," and handed him the final pair.

"Why are you giving me these?" he asked respectfully.

"I'm visiting from Australia and thought you might like something Aussie for next time you go swimming at the beach."

"Thank you." He seemed like a quiet person. He probably had a lot on his mind as he'd been called up from the minor leagues and wanted to perform well and stay at the top level. He didn't play on September 17, but was given the start at centre field and batted lead-off on September 18, where he collected three hits in five at-bats. When I saw Dyson's hustle, his talent shone rays of immense potential which could contribute to helping the team win.

The Indians dominated the game on September 17, breaking away in the fourth inning with four unanswered runs in that inning alone. It was Shin-Soo Choo's night as he hit three home runs for the Indians, including a grand slam, giving the Indians an 11–4 victory. It must have been those Australian board shorts I gave him! Despite both teams being out of the playoffs race, 21,168 people attended the game.

It was a much closer game on September 18, but the game was delayed by rain, causing a late finish with the Indians again winning, this time 6–4, in front of a crowd of 18,112 people. I got back to my hotel in the early hours of September 19 and was too tired to go to the game that night. With the benefit of hindsight I shouldn't have been so soft, as I didn't leave Kansas City until September 21, giving me plenty of time to catch up on sleep.

My wonderful experience with the Kansas City Royals didn't end on September 18. On September 20, the Royals were up in Detroit playing the Tigers, and Australian left-handed pitcher Brad Thomas came into the game. Thomas was in the midst of his best year in the US, having made his Major League debut with the Minnesota Twins on May 26, 2001. Royals Radio Network Announcer Steve Stewart's broadcast call included the following:

> Brad Thomas formally a Minnesota Twin and a breaking ball misses outside. We had an Aussie in the home radio booth this weekend, our friend Nicholas Henning,

> the author, former pro-baseball player over in Australia, written a couple of books, loves the game of baseball, had a great time at Kauffman Stadium. Here's the pitch, swing and a tapper foul. He wrote *Boomerang Baseball*, is his latest work, and before that *The American Dream: From Perth to Sacramento*, about an Australian ballplayer coming over to play in the US, and yes they're on Amazon.com, he'd want us to tell you.

It is impossible for me to express how grateful I am to Steve Stewart for mentioning me whilst calling a game, but what I can say is that it is further proof of how welcoming and generous Americans are with visiting Aussie baseball enthusiasts.

To be mentioned in the same sentence as Brad Thomas is one of my greatest baseball achievements to date. On September 20, two Australians had a win, as Thomas was the winning pitcher of record for the Tigers, in their 7–5 victory and I had been given another massive break as an Aussie baseball author.

There is one point that needs correction, though. I have never been a professional baseball player. The misunderstanding probably came from a previous discussion where I had mentioned to Steve playing baseball in the Sydney Major League, which is true, and the league does have collegiate and professional players, but plenty of amateurs like me. Also, in the US the term Major League is always associated with professional sports.

At the start of the 2010 Major League Baseball season, Brad Thomas would have set himself many goals and I'm sure he was determined to do a good job and help his team win games. Well, his statistics for the season certainly confirmed he had a successful year with six wins and two losses giving him a .750 winning percentage, an ERA of 3.89, he appeared in 49 games, pitching 69.1 innings and struck out 30 batters.

I'd seen Thomas pitch as a teenager for the Sydney Blues in the former Australian Baseball League, during the 1995/1996 season, where Sydney won the ABL Championship Series. He had actually made his ABL debut during the 1994/1995 season, appearing in just one game, pitching 0.2 innings, and giving up three earned runs, leaving him with an ERA of 40.50. But just one year later his season numbers saw him appear in five games for two wins and no losses with an ERA of 2.45 over 14.2 innings pitched.

Yet I remember him for pitching the Sydney Blues into the Championship Series, with his solid work on the mound in game three, which was the decider of the playoff series against the Perth Heat, on February 11, 1996. The starting pitcher for the Blues that night got knocked around a little, pitching one complete inning for three runs, but only one was earned. Brad Thomas then pitched eight innings against a lethal Heat batting line-up, giving up only two earned runs, to keep Sydney in the game and veteran Sydney reliever Karl Hardman pitched the tenth inning, giving up just one hit to seal the win for Sydney.

I have met Thomas a few times and thrown with him on one occasion during the Australian summer of 2004/2005, when I was playing for North Shore in the Sydney Major League. He knew a few people on our team and wanted to do some training during the American off-season to keep his arm in shape. To think we would be connected in a radio game call, during a US Major League Baseball game, is a thought I could not have imagined when I saw him play in the ABL or when I met him for the first time. Thanks to Don Free and Steve Stewart, it happened.

Brad Thomas deserves special mention as his career has included playing professional baseball in many countries. He pitched for the Australian baseball team at the Sydney 2000 Summer Olympic Games and played in many other international tournaments, including the 2009 World Baseball Classic. He had stints playing Major League Baseball with the Minnesota Twins from 2001–2004, from 2005–2006 he played Nippon Professional Baseball in Japan with the Hokkaido Nippon Ham Fighters and from 2008–2009 he played for the Hanwha Eagles in the Korean Baseball Organization. All of that experience paid dividends for him with his 2010 season on a very competitive Detroit Tigers team. As of 2010, he was one of just a few Australians to have played at the top level in the US, Korea, and Japan, with Chris Oxspring coming to mind as another member of this fraternity.

Yet it is an experience off the field that is one of his most miraculous stories. On September 11, 2001, Thomas and his future wife Kylie were scheduled to be on American Airlines Flight 11 from Boston to Los Angeles. Tragically, this flight was hijacked and crashed into the North Tower of the World Trade Center in New York City. At the time, Thomas was playing AA minor league baseball with the New Britain Rock Cats in Connecticut. Had it not been for two home runs from future Twins slugger Michael Cuddyer during the playoff series, which allowed the Rock Cats to progress to the Eastern League Championship, Thomas and his partner would have been on that flight. It is profound that Cuddyer's excellent skills as a baseball player saved the life of his teammate and his future wife. Thomas and Cuddyer already had a bond as friends who roomed together during various stages of their baseball careers, but their bond has been fused forever as two lives were saved by two brilliant swings of Cuddyer's baseball bat.

My flight departed Kansas City at 6:00 a.m., on September 21, flying on American Airlines AA1633 to Dallas/Fort Worth, Texas, which was a backward route to my next stop in Charleston, South Carolina. From Dallas/Fort Worth International Airport, I departed at 8:20 a.m. on American Airlines AA2827 (operated by American Eagle) to Charleston International Airport. I spent some time during my flights thinking of my friends Don Free and Steve Stewart and feeling immensely grateful, hoping one day they might venture to Australia so I could show them Sydney. But until that day comes, e-mails, Australian postcards, the occasional phone call, and some packets of Tim Tams posted from Australia would have to be my way of letting them know I'm thinking of them.

I arrived at Charleston International Airport at 11:55 a.m. Charleston didn't have a baseball theme for me, but it was a chance to see a part of America overseas travellers sometimes miss. Charleston has lots of waterways and beaches close by, and it seemed like a great place to catch some sun and swim before my next baseball stop of Washington DC.

CHAPTER 3
THE WASHINGTON DC NATIONALS

On September 24, 2010, I departed Charleston, South Carolina, at 10:11 a.m. on United UA7135 (Operated by United Express/Atlantic Southeast Airlines). Anytime a plane ticket says operated by someone else, it means expect a smaller, crappier plane, with even worse food. The flight only took an hour and a half to reach Washington Dulles International and I booked a taxi van to my hotel, the Capitol Skyline.

My long cricket bags drew some attention from a teenage passenger and his mother. "Do you play ball?" the mother had turned and asked me as I got comfortable in the back seat. Her son was probably in his late teens as he had a few whiskers on his chin. He had this excited look on his face as though he was expecting me to say I was a professional baseball player and ask for an autograph. Sometimes I really wish I was a pro baseball player because people look at you differently and even though it's nice to feel special, I couldn't go along with it, instead I replied, "There's an Aussie pitching for the Atlanta Braves who might come into the game tonight against the Nationals. I've travelled from Australia to watch some baseball and hopefully see Aussie Peter Moylan pitch for the Braves."

There was a slight drop in their faces for a split second, yet their smiles tilted straight back up hearing my Australian accent. From that point on, all they talked about was how much they want to visit Australia and they asked dozens of questions about the Land Down Under, which included plenty of kangaroo chat.

I was the last passenger to be dropped off, as all the others alighted north or southeast of the north-western sections of Constitution Avenue. My accommodation was basically southwest, but there was genius to my location as all I had to do was turn right on the street of my hotel, I Street South West, and then turn right again onto South Capitol Street and head down to the southeast end and Nationals Park was on the left hand side! I didn't have trendy fashion shops or restaurants, but I had baseball, and that's all I needed.

My hotel was government grey on the outside with rectangular windows from top to bottom. Whilst it wasn't a sexy building on the outside, it was reasonably jazzed up on the inside with loud, coloured cushions on the foyer lounges and energetic wallpaper around the place. My room had some mood to it with a lively coloured quilt and bright decorative pillows. There was a framed print on the wall of all the US presidents up until President George W. Bush. I had a great view of Capitol Hill from the window of my room, but with the day sneaking deeper into the afternoon, I decided to walk up to Nationals Park and buy a ticket for the game against the Braves.

As I only planned to watch one game of baseball in DC, I decided I would splash out a little. For $170, I would be able to watch the game close to home plate in section 123, row E, seat 1. The game didn't start for quite a few hours, and the gates hadn't even opened for the public to enter the field, so I decided to walk back to my hotel, have a shower, and put on some fresh clothes.

I think a lot when I walk and I began to link Aussies to the Nationals. It was made easier by the fact Major League Baseball moved the Montreal Expos to Washington DC and named them the Nationals at the conclusion of the 2004 season. Two Australians had played for the Expos. South Australian right-handed pitcher Shayne Bennett became the first Australian to debut at the Major League level with the Expos on August 22, 1997 and spent his entire Major League career with the Expos from 1997–1999. His final game was on August 15, 1999. The year 1998 was his biggest year as he appeared in sixty-two games with 91.2 innings pitched. Graeme Lloyd also pitched with the Expos from 2001–2002.

Whilst his Major League experience was certainly a wonderful career highlight for Bennett, some of his less well-known achievements were worthy of praise too. From 1993/1994–1998/1999, he played in the Australian Baseball League with the Adelaide Giants and Gold Coast Cougars. He started and ended with the Giants but had two seasons in-between with the Cougars. The fact he made himself available for ABL duties during the same period of time when he was playing in the Majors confirmed his wholehearted dedication to baseball in Australia.

Bennett also represented Australia at several international baseball tournaments. Yet the one which stands out most for me was the Sydney 2000 Summer Olympic Games. On September 17, 2000, he pitched in Australia's round-robin game against the Netherlands, and on September 22, 2000, he pitched in Australia's round-robin game against baseball powerhouse Cuba—his start against Cuba should be remembered as one of the best pitching performances by any Australian at an Olympic Games. He pitched 7.2 innings for only one earned run, and he struck out four batters. The final score was Cuba one, Australia zero, but Australia further proved itself as a highly competitive baseball country, and Bennett did an outstanding job keeping Australia in that game.

As of the 2010 season, Chris Snelling was the first and only Australian to have played Major League Baseball for the Nationals. Born in North Miami, Florida, Snelling's parents are Australian and the family relocated to Australia when he was still a boy.

Most Australians who have played Major League Baseball have been pitchers and plenty have made opening-day rosters, but few Aussies have achieved this as position players. Chris Snelling made the opening day roster for the Nationals on April 2, 2007, and was in the starting line up as the left fielder, which all adds up to be a historical breakthrough for an Australian on a Nationals team. The Nationals traded Snelling to the Oakland Athletics on May 2, 2007, for Ryan Langerhans. Ironically, San Antonio, Texas–born Langerhans has his own connection to Australia. Following the cessation of the first ABL venture was the International Baseball League of Australia, which Langerhans participated in during the 2000/2001 season. The green and yellow team colours of the Athletics are similar to Australia's green and gold national sporting colours, plus the green A's cap looks a lot like Aussie sports paraphernalia. Snelling made more history by becoming the first Australian to reach the Majors with the A's. In 2008, he appeared in four games for the Philadelphia Phillies, and in four at-bats he hit a double and a home run. His Major League career spanned from 2002–2008 and he played his final game at this level on June 6, 2008.

Snelling had super talent, but injuries shortened his career. Notwithstanding, he was a gifted player who played well beyond his age and this was evident even in Australia. During the 1997/1998 ABL season, he debuted with the Hunter Eagles, appearing in eight games; four games were starts, and he cracked one hit that happened to be a home run. It is important to be mindful Snelling celebrated his sixteenth birthday on December 3, 1997. Snelling played the 1998/1999 ABL season with the Sydney Storm, where he played in twenty-one games and knocked out a batting average of .257 with three home runs. He was the youngest baseball player at the Sydney 2000 Summer Olympic Games at eighteen years and 289 days old. Snelling truly had a knack for belting home runs and became the youngest Australian to hit a home run at the Major League level at twenty years old, achieving this playing for the Seattle Mariners on May 29, 2002. He was called up to the Majors on May 25, collecting his first Major League hit on May 28 and in his twelfth career at-bat on May 29 he went deep. Snelling should be remembered for his power hitting. His 1.500 slugging percentage during limited action with the Phillies in 2008 and multiple home runs on behalf of Australia at the 2009 World Baseball Classic, confirm he was a gifted hitter from the start to the end of his professional career.

I ventured back to Nationals Park with plenty of time left before the game started, feeling fresh after having a hot shower and putting on clean clothes. I made a pit stop at McDonalds and as I approached the gates to the field they were open! The Atlanta Braves were still going through their batting practice session as I strolled in feeling excited to be experiencing a new Major League ballpark and witness another game. The Braves have a notable history in Australia, which made national sporting news headlines, when they signed Glenn Williams at the age of sixteen on August 17, 1993. Williams was a prodigy for his age as a slick infielder and solid hitter, but it was his signing bonus that left the Australian sports media in a spin. He is reported to have signed for $925,000 US, which at the time converted to about $1.3 million AUD. High expectations were placed on his career, and he made his Major League debut with the Minnesota Twins on June 7, 2005, and played his final game at that level on June 28, 2005.

Three Australians had played Major League Baseball with the Braves as of 2010. Damian Moss was the first Australian to debut with the Braves, on April 26, 2001 and he played some of his best baseball as a Brave. Peter Moylan followed on April 12, 2006 and then Phil Stockman on June 15, 2006. There must have been a few packets of Tim Tams in the Braves' front office during the 2006 season with two Australians debuting in such quick succession. Stockman played his last Major League game as a Brave on June 11, 2008. He is part of a rare group of players to have played in both versions of the ABL and he was also on the Australian baseball team which finished with a silver medal at the 2004 Athens Summer Olympic Games. Stockman appeared in the round-robin game against Chinese Taipei on August 16, 2004; Australia's round-robin win against Japan on August 18, 2004, where he pitched 4.1 innings and struck out four batters; and the game against Canada on August 22, 2004.

As I walked toward the left field stand and looked down into the Braves' bullpen, I couldn't see Moylan. I scanned the field and realised he was close to the infield helping collect balls during the batting practice session. Even at the Major League level, it is pleasing to see how the whole team has a responsibility when it comes to training, regardless of whether they bat or not in games. I didn't realise at the time how lucky I was, but out of all the players who happened to be in the bullpen about to head out to the field, the one to catch my attention was Eric O'Flaherty. Unknown to me was that O'Flaherty had an Aussie connection, having previously played with the Seattle Mariners when Chris Snelling and Travis Blackley played there. That probably explained when I called out, "Hey, mate, can you do a favour for me?" He looked up. I added, "Could you please tell Peter Moylan the guy who wrote Australia's first baseball novel would like to quickly speak with him? I'm the author of two Aussie baseball-themed books."

"Sure, I'll let him know."

"Thanks, mate."

He gave me a wave as if to say "No worries" and walked onto the field.

I could see O'Flaherty talking with Moylan and they were looking in my direction. I suddenly wished I had a couple of packets of Tim Tams to give O'Flaherty for relaying my message. Moylan raised his arms above his head to get my attention. He waved and pointed to the bullpen I was standing above. It was clear he was indicating he would talk with me at the bullpen after he finished what he was doing.

I had posted, care of the Atlanta Braves, a copy of my book *The American Dream: From Perth to Sacramento* to Moylan during the 2009 season. It hadn't been sent back to me, so I assumed he had probably received it. As I watched the batting practice session, I again reminded myself good fortune had a habit of going my way on this trip. If it wasn't for the kind heartedness of O'Flaherty I might have been standing there feeling frustrated about getting Moylan's attention.

The Braves wrapped up their batting practice session, and Moylan walked back toward the bullpen. I suddenly wondered what I would say to him. He looked up and said, "How's it going?"

"Great! My name's Nick Henning, I wrote Australia's first baseball novel, *The American Dream: From Perth to Sacramento* and I posted you a copy last year. Did you receive it okay?"

"No, I didn't get that."

I felt embarrassed and a bit disappointed the book hadn't reached him.

"I'll send you another copy, but what's the best way to do this?"

"If you send it by FedEx, it will be delivered to my locker."

"I'll organise a copy for you."

"So what brings you here?"

"I'm here to see you pitch."

"We'll see if I get into the game. Thanks for the support, though."

"You're doing great work for the Braves and baseball in Australia."

"Thanks, I've got to get going, but have a great trip." My holiday was becoming stacked with great memories and having spoken with two Aussie Major Leaguers I wondered if it could get any better. An inner voice told me it would.

Moylan is a unique, colourful, and inspiring Australian baseball story. He was signed by the Minnesota Twins as an amateur free agent on January 28, 1996, as a seventeen-year-old. He played two years of rookie ball, with an ERA of 4.08 for the 1996 minor league season and 4.05 for 1997. His statistics were close to midrange for a relief pitcher, but he also started seven games during the 1997 season, which indicated the organisation felt he had potential to be a starting pitcher. The Twins released him on April 1, 1998, and at eighteen years old he had to consider life after professional baseball. Moylan had played in the ABL with the Perth Heat during the 1996/1997 and 1997/1998 seasons. His ERA was 6.23 for '96/'97 and 6.00 for '97/'98, which were competitive but not convincing numbers. Perhaps still determined to be a professional baseball player, he crossed Australia and joined the Sydney Storm for the 1998/1999 season. With an ERA of 7.62 and the demise of the first version of the ABL, it seemed Moylan might have to be content with just playing baseball for fun.

The journey Moylan took after 1999 should be ranked as one of Australia's greatest sporting stories, yet it is only known in local Aussie baseball circles and amongst Braves faithful fans. Not even twenty years old, he had to consider life after baseball and reconnect himself with normal life, and he found a job as a pharmaceutical salesman in Australia. As time went on, he had a family. So he just played baseball for fun, yet he had enough talent to earn a spot on the Victorian Claxton Shield team. His pitching arm was sore more often than he wanted, so he hit and played some first base. Perhaps a flash of genius came over Moylan, or maybe it was a stubborn refusal to accept his pitching days were over, but he reinvented his pitching delivery to sidearm/submarine style. Moylan quickly found himself on the Australian 2006 World Baseball Classic team with a fastball clocked at 96 mph. He turned heads when he struck out respected players Bobby Abreu and Magglio Ordonez, both of whom were noted for their formidable hitting at the Major League level in the US. But the quantum leap was far from over when he signed with the Braves on March 10, 2006 and made his Major League debut on April 12, 2006. His statistics up to 2010 were highly impressive. His ERA for 2007 was 1.80, during the 2009 season it was 2.84, and for 2010 he finished with 2.97. An injury cost him most of 2008. Moylan was highly regarded in the Braves' bullpen, and his success was enjoyable to keep track of. There have been some whispers of an Australian baseball film, and Moylan's career certainly ticks all the right boxes.

As I stood there thinking about Australian baseball growth opportunities through film, I noticed one of the Nationals coaching staff had Radison and the number 53 on his shirt. Then it clicked: the Nationals Manager was Jim Riggleman, and Radison had also been on his coaching staff with the San Diego Padres from 1993–1994 and the Chicago Cubs from 1995–1999. There was no mistake; it was the same Dan Radison who was the manager of the Brisbane Bandits in the Australian Baseball League. The Bandits won the ABL championship with him as manager in 1993/1994, and he had a super Bandits team for 1995/1996 with Dave Nilsson and Graeme Lloyd both on the roster. It was a spin out to be in America and to see Radison coaching at the Major League level.

As game time approached, I settled into my seat. The field was beautiful. The right field lights and scoreboard caught my attention with powerful white luminosity shining down onto the field, and decorating the scoreboard in red neon, the team logo and name sparkled more and more in the darkening night sky.

I have been fortunate enough to see so many talented baseball players take the field at Major League games in the US, yet Ivan "Pudge" Rodriguez is in a special category because I can say I saw one of the best catchers of all time. It is always a matter of opinion as to who is regarded as baseball's greatest catcher, and many different eras need to be considered, but there is no doubt in my mind Pudge is the finest catcher of his generation.

When he made his Major League debut with the Texas Rangers on June 20, 1991, he was only nineteen years old. The year 2010 marked his twentieth year in the Major Leagues and he played the majority of his career as a Texas Ranger, but he had played on six different Major League clubs during his career. He is a certain Baseball Hall of Fame inductee as his achievements in the game cover so many categories, including: selection as an All-Star fourteen times; named the American League Most Valuable Player for the 1999 season; a member of the Florida Marlins 2003 World Series champion team; over 300 career home runs; a career batting average just under .300; and as of 2010, almost 3,000 career hits. Whilst there are no doubt numerous North Americans who would love to see Pudge play live, I could only imagine I was part of a rare group of Aussie baseball fans to have sat only metres away from him. To see him catch behind the plate ranks high amongst all my baseball experiences. He cracked a base hit during the game against the Braves, and I was one of 22,515 fans to have seen another hit in his stellar career.

The Nationals bashed the Braves out of the game early with three runs by the bottom of the third. The final score of 8–3 contained plenty of heavy hitting, with the Nationals' Adam Dunn blasting two home runs and Nationals outfielder Willie Harris sprinting out an inside-the-park-home run with lightning speed. If there are baseball gods, they certainly answered my prayers as Peter Moylan came into the game to close out the fifth inning. His job was to get one out, as Tim Hudson had pitched 5.2 innings and that's exactly what he did for no damage. My wish to see a second Aussie pitch at the Major League level came true that night.

I had three more nights in Washington and I could have seen some more baseball games, but I chose to be a tourist instead. The District of Columbia is only 177 square kilometres in size, yet a person can easily be occupied for days on end just by visiting all the sites around Constitution Avenue and Independence Avenue. The White House, Lincoln Memorial, Smithsonian Institution museums, US Capitol, and the Washington Monument all make for fantastic walking tours.

The Vietnam Veterans Memorial took me by surprise. The shiny black granite V-shaped walls list 58,256 Americans who lost their lives during the conflict and the names are in order from the first to the last casualty of war. A directory book onsite, which is as thick as a telephone book, has all the names in alphabetical order and I suddenly wondered if a Henning had lost their life in Vietnam. I had been to the National War Memorial in Canberra and did not find a Henning who had lost their life defending Australia in any war. It's not such a common name and in Sydney it only takes up a few lines in the phone book. But names flashed out on the page: Arthur R. Henning and Douglas A. Henning. I became filled with thoughts, as the possibility of being related to these men was an intriguing prospect. I quickly realised the surname Henning has been in America a lot longer than it has in Australia and these men could only be very distant relatives at best, yet I somehow felt connected to them despite only sharing a name.

I took some time to sit at a nearby park bench and think in the quiet and clear warm weather—and then it came to me easily, as though I was always meant to be there that day. Perhaps it will only ever be an idea, but I became engrossed with the thought of writing a book about these two men.

They would probably still have relatives I could interview and their military records could be obtained. It is the normal people behind their service and ultimate sacrifice I want to represent most and capture memories from family, friends, and comrades. If the day comes when writing becomes my full-time occupation, putting together their story is one of my highest priorities. They both came from different states in America so it is likely they weren't related. It's so tempting to start researching and gathering information now. In the next couple of years, I might just do that.

I had a morning flight on September 28. This time I left from Ronald Reagan National Airport, which was a quick taxi trip from my hotel. American Airlines AA4440 (operated by American Eagle) departed at 9:25 a.m. The flight time to John F. Kennedy International Airport in New York was just one hour and five minutes. The thought of New York City gave me an instant spark, as I looked forward to exploring the vast metropolis, seeing more baseball games, catching up with friends, and being a tourist.

CHAPTER 4
THE NEW YORK METS

I arrived at JFK International Airport right on time at 10:30 a.m. Despite its considerable size, I felt like I made fairly quick progress. I booked a taxi van, and a thrill came over me knowing I was about to step into a city I knew of through so many different scenes in movies and television programs.

As expected, there was plenty of traffic on the road and my hotel, the Holiday Inn Express on Wall Street, was the last stop, as I had chosen to stay in lower Manhattan. Even though it wasn't the busiest time of the day to be on the road, it was slow going once we got close to Broadway. I decided September 28 would be the day I would just wander around. I didn't have a lot of time in New York, as I flew out on October 1, so I wanted to make sure the two full days I had there were well used. The weather was a bit of a worry though, with severe rain warnings. I just hoped the rain would stay away for September 30, as I would be attending a New York Mets versus Milwaukee Brewers game and meeting friends. The rain wasn't such a worry for September 29 because I planned to visit the Empire State Building.

By the time I reached my hotel, only about an arm's reach from Wall Street, it was afternoon. I wanted to make good use of the daylight I still had available so I set about on a self-guided walking tour, having only glanced at a map in the hotel lobby. Being so close to City Hall, Wall Street, the Federal Reserve Bank, and the New York Stock Exchange, I felt I had enough bearings to find my way back, plus this area of lower Manhattan is slightly downhill, so that also gave me a sense of direction.

Even though I had never visited New York City, I knew I was fairly close to Ground Zero of the World Trade Center site, as I had seen so much of the area on television following the September 11, 2001, terrorist attacks. The afternoon was warm, yet a cold chill came over me when I suddenly felt compelled to visit the site. I was half a world away when the attacks happened, yet I would learn the events of that day were much closer to me than I first realised. News of the event reached Australia live, but it wasn't until morning when I got in my car and turned on the radio for the drive to work from Chatswood to Parramatta that I became aware of what had happened. At first I didn't believe what I was hearing. The Nova 96.9 morning crew of Merrick and Rosso often humoured me into a workday, and even though they spoke with serious tones, it took a few minutes to realise I was hearing the frightening truth. I felt numb and that evening on the television news, the images became engraved in my mind forever.

Ten Australians are known to have died in the September 11 attacks. It became apparent two of the deceased could have easily passed me in the street or stood next to me. Alberto Dominguez from Lidcombe, in suburban Sydney, was sixty-six years old and a few weeks off from retiring as a Qantas Airways baggage handler. He was on American Airlines Flight 11, which was flown into the North Tower of the World Trade Center. It was the same flight Brad and Kylie Thomas were scheduled to have been on but cancelled because of the extension of Brad's baseball season. It is possible when I caught the train from Merrylands Station to the city Alberto Dominguez might have boarded the same train as me, further down the line at Lidcombe, as I caught the train from Merrylands between 1996 to 2000, often going through the city or getting off at Strathfield Station to change trains. Alberto's grandson Jamie was only a month old when the attacks happened, and the Dominguez family congregated at a son's home in Greystanes, just one suburb from Merrylands, when they were trying to learn of their father's situation.

Stephen K. Tompsett was a computer scientist and vice president of technology for Instinet Corp, an electronics equity brokerage. The thirty-nine-year-old from my own suburb of Merrylands had lived in New York for over ten years with his American wife and daughter. His parents still lived in Merrylands, and it was noted in various news reports Tompsett often returned to Australia with his family. I could have walked past or stood next to Tompsett at the local shops or in Central Gardens in Merrylands West and never known it. On September 11, he was attending a technology conference at the restaurant on the top floor of the World Trade Center North Tower.

My dad, Roger Henning, has the closest connection to the September 11 attacks of any person I know. One of his best friend's, Larry Wong, lost his girlfriend, Betty Ann Ong. She is considered a hero of September 11, as she was a flight attendant on American Airlines Flight 11 and made a twenty-three-minute call to the airline during the hijacking. Ong provided the seat numbers of the hijackers, which confirmed their identities. She also described the events that were taking place and the names of crew and passengers who were injured as the hijackers took control of the plane. My dad had spoken with Ong only a few weeks before as he planned to catch up with her and Larry later that year.

Dad had spent years working as a crisis management consultant. He had been crisis manager after the Port Arthur Massacre, which occurred on the Tasman Peninsula, south-east of Hobart (Tasmania, Australia) on April 28, 1996, when a gunman opened fire on tourists, leaving thirty-five dead and many others injured. I didn't make the connection at the time, but Dad made a sudden career change in the wake of the September 11 attacks, becoming a consultant and director specialising in airport security and anti-terrorism security technologies. I have no doubt the loss of Betty Ong contributed to his decision to concentrate the remaining years of his career on preventing terrorism.

It might have been easier for me to not visit Ground Zero, but my mind was determined to go. I walked to the Tribute World Trade Center and Fire Department New York Engine 10. New construction was well underway, and various foundations had been laid. The bones of the future were still too naked to look at as profound emptiness swept over me. The sense of loss was unavoidable with the dreary, empty sky, the miserable concrete grey edifice, and shadows from surrounding buildings adding to the bleakness. A wall featuring photographs of the faces of fire crew who lost their lives stared at me and the gaze of so many fathers, brothers, uncles, and friends was a shock wave that left me swaying uneasy on me feet. I was only there for a matter of minutes, yet it was so overwhelming I had to leave before nearby people saw the tears in my eyes.

I spent the rest of that afternoon and evening walking and found comfort at Battery Park and nearby areas, hearing the joy in other tourists' voices and seeing their smiles as they departed and returned from Liberty and Ellis Island. Their happiness was a helpful medicine. I didn't have dinner and went to sleep within minutes of having a shower and getting comfortable in my warm bed.

I woke up on September 29, 2010, feeling refreshed and eager to visit the Empire State Building, but decided to book a night ticket and use the day to do more exploring. I began the morning by crossing boroughs, taking a decent walk from my hotel and over the Brooklyn Bridge. So many tourists from around the world had taken the exact same steps as me. When the 2000 Baseball World Series was a subway series between the Mets and Yankees, I remember between innings seeing shots of the cityscape and a nice close up of the Brooklyn Bridge. I never thought one day I would walk across the famous suspension bridge. I enjoyed the fresh air and view so much I walked back across to Manhattan so I could have a two-way experience rather than take the subway back.

It was a good thing I was wearing sneakers and sports socks because I walked all the way up to Central Park. I laughed remembering scenes from the television shows *Seinfeld* and *Sex and the City*, which were filmed on location there. I spent most of the afternoon in the park and lay on my back in the grass just watching the world spin.

My tickets to the Empire State Building Observatory and the 102nd floor cost me $35. I actually thought it might be more expensive than that and was pleasantly surprised. The queuing takes some time and effort, but for one of the best views in New York City it's worth the labour. The evening lights were just starting to glow in the remnants of daytime. Central Park appeared as a stark natural contrast to the forest of buildings that surrounded it on all four sides. The rows of buildings looked never ending and stood as proof of copious man-hours of construction and the millions of people who call New York City home. As evening started to take stronger hold, Times Square looked like a shining treasure boxed in by tall buildings. I could have stayed up there all night as the peacefulness was so relaxing and the view around me changed with different lights going on and the movement of ant-like traffic. I knew I couldn't stay out too late as I had baseball to look forward to the next day and I still needed to make my way back down to my hotel.

September 30 was all for baseball, but severe rain and winds had been looming since the day of my arrival. I hoped the weather wouldn't get in the way of my plans, and lucky for me it didn't. As of 2010, two Australians had played for the New York Mets. The first was Craig Shipley in 1989, followed by Graeme Lloyd in 2003. I was pleased David Newman, senior vice president of marketing and communications for the Mets, had responded to my correspondence regarding my first baseball novel. I hoped to catch up with him for lunch while I was there, but the weather and his stacked timetable made it difficult to fit it in. I purchased four tickets for the game that day, which were for three guests and me. Perhaps it was intuition, but I had a feeling that I would one day ask David for a favour. I didn't think about it too much at the time, yet in early 2011 my good friend Nick Moll told me of his plans to travel to New York with his wife Elizabeth and hopefully catch a Mets game.

Nick is the most loyal Mets fan I know, and despite some very bumpy seasons during the early 1990s, his support for them has never wavered. His visit was like a pilgrimage and more than two decades in the making. I felt excited for him that he was finally going to see his team play in New York.

When he was a child, he had visited America on a family holiday and he was a credit card swipe away from having his own fitted Mets cap when his dad's card didn't work for the transaction. So I told David that Nick was coming and asked if there was any chance he could extend some hospitality to the Molls. David appreciated the journey Nick had taken to get there and his loyalty to the team. He kindly organised some tickets for both of them. April 14, 2011, was a special day for Nick and Elizabeth as they watched the Mets take on the Colorado Rockies. David's assistant Carrie Kwok came and spoke with them in their seats and discussed their visit to New York and Citi Field. David and Carrie both contributed to Nick fulfilling a sporting dream and it is continuously evident, based on my own experiences and Nick's, that American generosity is exceptional. I'm pleased I was able to play a small part in Nick's ability to see the Mets play. I told him to have some Tim Tams on hand to give away. During that trip, he finally purchased himself a fitted Mets cap and numerous other baseball items.

Back to September 30, 2010. I was meeting for the first time Long Island, New York, journalist Chris R. Vaccaro. I also had a ticket for his girlfriend Theresa and her younger sister Melissa. I came to know Chris when he was working as a freelance journalist for the *Massapequa Post*. As this is a suburban publication, I felt Chris would be more likely to receive a copy of my first baseball book which I sent to him, and that he might take an interest in it. He did, and we have been mates since 2009.

There were specific reasons I picked a newspaper in Massapequa and chose Chris. His surname had been around me for many years as a Vaccaro Group Electrical and Air Conditioning van always caught my eye as I turned right from Brian Street onto Lucy Street in Merrylands West. To this day, the van is probably parked in a driveway on Lucy Street. Also, his name sounded sporty and seemed to fit my perceived mould of a promising American media identity. In addition, the hamlet of Massapequa became ingrained in my memory because of the film and book *Born on the Fourth of July*, which is based on the life of American Vietnam veteran Ron Kovic.

There were clouds in the sky on the afternoon of September 30 and I worried the game might be delayed by showers or potentially rained out. Thankfully the weather was kind. I took the number seven train to the Mets/Willets Point Station, but it was far from simple. Being in a foreign country always adds a bit of extra anxiety and the whole process probably wasn't too complicated, but in my mind it was. I was petrified of getting on the wrong train and ending up in the complete opposite direction. Also, not all the metro stops had station attendants so I had to ask other commuters how to buy a ticket and what I needed to do. It was a nice old lady who assisted me. "Now don't worry, kid, you pay for usage as opposed to a cost from A to B." She put my money into a ticket machine and said, "This will get you there and back and go Mets!" She had a sweet smile on her face the whole time and explained to me I could connect to the seven from Grand Central Terminal. It's a blur remembering which station I even got on at, but everything centred around Grand Central and suddenly I had it reasonably worked out in my head. I was visiting a new borough too, as I was venturing into Queens for the first time. I smirked, thinking to myself I could visit George Costanza's parents from *Seinfeld* in Queens.

I met Chris, Theresa, and Melissa at the Mets home run red apple, which is on a little grass island between the train station stairs and Citi Field. I waited nervously because I was meeting a pen pal, or in this day of Internet technology an e-pal, for the first time. I wondered if he would recognise me. As I waited, I enjoyed looking at the exterior of the stadium with its wonderful blend of the old and the new. The different tones of the brickwork and the tall terracotta bricked window arches caught my attention. I had Tim Tams and Cadbury chocolate on hand. By this point, I had made it a tradition that no first meeting between an Aussie and an American could be complete without these delicacies. Chris would later tell me he ate all of the Tim Tams during his drive home that night and the chocolate only made it a few minutes into the journey before the three of them had eaten it all. Chris normally isn't fond of chocolate, but he enjoyed the Aussie version and loved the Tim Tams. I also had a pair of Aussie flag board shorts for him, but the size wasn't right and he gave them to his younger brother Bryan.

The three of them walked straight toward me and Chris, the faithful Mets fan, had his cap and a supporters playing shirt on, with sandy coloured long shorts, and both Theresa and Melissa were wearing black Mets T-shirts and dark blue jeans. I felt a connection with all of them straightaway as we talked easily and my big trip across America was the topic of plenty of conversation.

The Mets were a shadow of themselves because of injuries to so many high profile players. Jason Bay and Carlos Beltran had succumbed to injury, just to name a few. However, I was pleased to see star shortstop Jose Reyes and ever-reliable David Wright at third base. Reyes went hitless in four at-bats and made a fielding error in the fifth inning, and Wright was steady with one hit from four at-bats.

The tickets I purchased for us were field level and fairly close to the dugout, in section 110, row 1, and seats 5 to 8. It was a nice spot to watch baseball from. Our closest fielding position was first base, which was great because slugger Prince Fielder was on the Brewers team. He didn't record a hit, but he was walked three times. The Mets pitchers were smart to frequently walk him, as he was a powerful hitter who could make one big swing hurt a lot.

The players were focused on their jobs on the field, but I did manage to get Prince Fielder's attention on one occasion. Late in the game, just as the infield warm up was about to finish, Fielder turned his head to the dugout, about to lob the ball in, when I suddenly leapt up in a star jump and yelled "Prince! Throw me the ball!" He must have heard me because he did and it was caught by a diving Chris, who risked injury and caused himself a bruise down one side of his body to catch it. A section usher made sure Chris was okay and offered to take him to a first aid officer, but Chris dusted himself off and declared, "I'm fine, I've got the ball!"

The final score in the game was Brewers nine, Mets two, and 24,661 people attended the game, which was a pretty good crowd as the Mets were well out of playoff contention and missing a lot of key personnel. We took some photographs after the game inside the stadium, and the field was so pretty. All the seating sections were neatly laid out, and I loved the big red neon Pepsi-Cola sign above the right field stand. Americans always keep history well connected; I wish we did more of that in Australia, because the Citi Field car park is where the old Shea Stadium was and they had marked the old home plate and the infield with steel markers. It was nice to stand there in the batter's box and think that Aussie Craig Shipley once stood in the exact same spot when he was playing with the Mets and Graeme Lloyd pitched from the mound spot. The list of Hall of Fame players who accumulated part of their career statistics on that field is extensive. Even though the field isn't there any more, it lives on with so many memories and great achievements, like the 1986 Mets World Series championship team.

Within walking distance from Citi Field is Flushing Meadows, the home of the US Open tennis championship. It is a popular event for Aussies as we've had some success in that annual Grand Slam tournament. Since the late 1990s, Australia has had a good run, with Pat Rafter winning the men's singles crown back to back in 1997 and 1998, followed by Lleyton Hewitt in 2001, and Sam Stosur won the women's singles crown in 2011.

Chris, Theresa, and Melissa drove home in Chris's black Dodge Nitro, a very cool car and I took the train back to Lower Manhattan. It was Chris who pointed out to me how close Flushing Meadows was to the field. As the night got later, the rain started to roll in and I felt even luckier my evening had gone the way it had. The silver trains looked the same from the *Crocodile Dundee* films, and I liked seeing an American flag painted on the side because national pride is something the Americans do well. We don't have Australian flags painted on the sides of trains at home, but I wish we did.

As had become ritual before leaving for a new destination, I packed up all my belongings and laid out what I was going to wear for a day of travel. I put my sneakers close to the bed and noticed a blue pill resting in a slim gully between the carpet and the under-bed tray which pulls out, where fresh sheets are stored for the room service staff. It came to me instantly! I had been sharing my room with a misplaced Viagra pill! A good time may not have been had by all because the fuel for "energy" had been lost. I wondered if they had searched the bed sheets frantically or combed the carpet looking for this super stimulant. Then I laughed, thinking of the possibilities. Was it an elderly couple holidaying in New York City, or was it a Wall Street fat cat too stressed out to perform naturally?

As I slept, the rain became so severe it woke me up during the early hours of October 1. Rain in Cleveland had caused delays to flights and it crossed my mind it could do the same to American Airlines AA19, due to depart from JFK at 10:30 a.m., bound for Los Angeles International Airport. I worried the morning traffic and the weather could cause me to be late. I didn't want to take any chances, so at 3:00 a.m. I jumped in the shower, got dressed, and checked out of my hotel. Reception called a taxi for me and little did I know I had actually made a very smart decision. The faster routes to JFK and the freeway were quickly flooding and I heard over the driver's radio a major pileup was causing entire road blockages. So we took the suburban route, I held on for dear life as the spray from cars driving on the other side of the road and alongside us splashed the taxi like waves. The force of the water was frightening as it slapped the metal panels of the car with a thud and obscured the windscreen for seconds at a time, despite the wipers going at maximum speed. We virtually came to a complete stop at various times and I have never been more scared on an urban road than I was that morning. I gave the driver a $20 tip.

I was several hours early for my flight, yet as the morning got underway, more and more announcements came over the public address system for passengers who hadn't yet checked in. With not much to do apart from watching some of the local morning news services, it became clear the severe weather had caused gridlock across the city by about 7:00 a.m. the time I had originally planned to leave my hotel.

October 1 certainly involved plenty of flying, with two flights totalling nearly nine hours, including crossing the US border into Vancouver, Canada. I visited my Canadian cousins, the Hacketts. My dad's sister Bronwyn had married Canadian Uncle Bruce, which made her an Aussie Maple Leaf and she had lived most of her life in Canada. I also caught up with some friends I made during a holiday to Barcelona in 2008. It was great to catch up with brothers Ross and Marten Hansen and Justin Nutt.

I stayed in Vancouver until October 5 and crossed the border, flying down to Portland, Oregon, to see my cousin Ben Raphael. His dad Jon was my mum's brother. Ben was married to Deena, who was American and they had made a nice home for themselves in Portland, with their two children Clara and Johnny. I spent a few days there and then flew down to Los Angeles on October 8.

From October 8–11, I put my feet up in Anaheim. I had planned to visit all the amusement parks and do various day tours, but felt too wiped to do anything much. I hardly even left the local area, but I was happy just to take it easy, as the flight of nearly fifteen hours back to Sydney on October 11 would be easier if I felt fresh and relaxed, which I did.

Even though I was heading back to Australia, there was baseball waiting for me, as the second incarnation of the Australian Baseball League was less than a month away.

CHAPTER 5
THE ABL 2010/2011

The return of the Australian Baseball League was a win for the game in the local sporting landscape. Since the demise of the previous ABL, which existed from Australia's 1989/1990 summer to 1998/1999, I had always hoped it would come back, yet a part of me felt it might never happen. Even when it was announced in July 2009 plans were underway to re-establish the ABL, I wanted to believe it but couldn't grasp it was actually going to happen. Much to my delight, it did. The last game played in the former ABL was game two of the 1998/1999 Championship Series between the Sydney Storm and the Gold Coast Cougars on February 13, 1999. The first game of the new ABL was played on November 6, 2010, between the Sydney Blue Sox and Canberra Cavalry.

I was nineteen years old and at the Sydney Showground the night the Gold Coast Cougars completed a sweep of the Sydney Storm two games to nil, in the three game series, to win the 1998/1999 ABL Championship. It never occurred to me it would be 4,284 days, or eleven years, eight months, and twenty-four days, between that day and the day the Sydney Blue Sox played the Canberra Cavalry on November 6, 2010. All those years later, I was thirty-one years old and the ABL was still a source of excitement.

With the reverse summers between North America and Australia, baseball fans could have double the fix and see some of Australia's best talent showcased. Unlike the Australian National Basketball League and A-League Football (soccer), the ABL season doesn't clash with overseas professional leagues such as Major League Baseball in North America. Television commercials on Foxtel featured some of Australia's Major League players saying "Baseball is back," and showed highlights of Team Australia winning, Australians playing in the Majors and even a clip of a local game played in Sydney. What attracted me most was the possibility of watching Aussie stars play on home soil. For years, I had followed their statistics and news items which featured them. To actually see them play was a baseball equivalent of waiting eleven years for Christmas. Some had played in local leagues and the Claxton Shield in between the two ABLs, but I hadn't taken much of an interest in either, so I would be seeing many players take the field for the first time.

Major League Baseball and the Australian Baseball Federation jointly owned the second version of the ABL. MLB has the majority share of the league. The ABL owned and governed all six teams, which was a shift away from the privately owned franchises of the previous venture. Without the support of MLB, it was doubtful the ABL would have been resurrected. It should never be forgotten MLB invested in the Major League Baseball Australian Academy Program (MLBAAP) on the Queensland Gold Coast, which was the most fertile training facility for young Australian players and also for players from Asia Pacific. Established in 2001, the MLBAAP had an impressive alumni of players who had gone on to play in the Majors, including Luke Hughes. During its first ten years the number of Australians playing US college or professional baseball rose by 40 per cent, and 80 per cent of all professional players went through the academy.

The international flavour to the new ABL also added plenty of excitement, with players from the US, Korea, Japan, Europe and some lesser known baseball countries such as India. Australians made up the majority of players across the league, yet it was exciting to see talent from all over the world in a forty-game regular season.

I didn't attend the opening game between the Sydney Blue Sox and the Canberra Cavalry on November 6, 2010, and regret not being there, due to a family commitment that night. I was there on November 12 and I didn't miss a single regular season home series at "Blue Town" Blacktown Olympic Park thereafter.

Both the Blue Sox and Cavalry had players on their rosters whose careers I had followed but had never seen play on home soil. Michael Collins was on the Cavalry team and I made it a priority to catch up with him. It was a credit to the ABL venues like Blue Town allowed access to the players after games. At over 1.9 metres tall, I had to look up to speak with him. With a long kit bag over one of his sturdy shoulders, I was able to talk with Collins for a few minutes. "Well done on attending your first Major League spring training with the Padres this year," I said as he walked toward me from the dugout field exit. Collins had accumulated ten years of minor league baseball, having begun his professional career playing rookie ball with the Angels at sixteen years old in 2001. He was only twenty-five, with his experience including parts of two seasons in AAA.

"Thank you," he replied earnestly and gave me his full attention, gratefully looking me in the eye as he slowly walked. I knew I had to say more while I had the chance and added,

"By the way, did you receive a copy of *The American Dream: From Perth to Sacramento* in the mail during the minor league season?"

"Yes, I did." He sounded surprised I would know about the book.

I said "I wrote that book," He seemed pleasantly surprised and gave me a convivial smile.

"I've read quite a bit of it, thank you for the copy." I had a proof copy of *Boomerang Baseball*, which is the copy before the first official one as I was out of spare copies that night. He struck me as a genuine guy. From what I've read about him within baseball circles, he's well liked, and turned heads at spring training by chalking up extra base hits in the Major League camp. "I want you to have this," I said, handing him the book, "this is my latest work and is actually the very first copy."

"Are you sure you want me to have this?"

"Absolutely, you've worked hard your whole career, you made yourself available to play for Australia at both World Baseball Classics and here in the ABL helping contribute to the new league."

"Thank you so much, I'll look after this." One of the Cavalry coaches called out to him, as their team bus was getting ready to go. "I've got to get going," he said, shaking my hand and wishing me well.

Collins was born in Canberra. He was one of the most talented players to have come out of the Australian Capital Territory. During the 2010/2011 season, he recorded the highest batting average, hitting a .360 and was a leader on a young Cavalry team.

It did come as a shock to me that an opportunity didn't eventuate for him during the 2011 US season, especially considering how well he played in the ABL. But baseball is a game and it's a business! Unfortunately there are times when the clubs run out of room within their organisations. However, baseball has continued on for Collins and he now coaches within professional ranks. With his vast playing experience and new career in coaching, he'll certainly continue to make an excellent contribution to the game abroad and within Australia. One day I hope he earns a spot on the Team Australia coaching staff.

Given the eleven-year absence between the two ABLs, it was rare to find many players who had stints in both. Michael Wells was on the Cavalry team and part of a small group of players to do that. He turned thirty-eight years old during the 2010/2011 season and brought with him a wealth of experience. From the 1991/1992 season to 1997/1998 season, he played for the Waverley Reds/Melbourne Reds, the Canberra Bushrangers and the Hunter Eagles. He was a reliable hitter and infielder. In 1997/1998, whilst playing for the Eagles he produced exceptional hitting statistics, with a batting average of .324 and sixteen home runs. He was twenty-five years old then and had played his career season. Yet with the demise of the Eagles, he chose not to play for another team in the ABL during the 1998/1999 season.

I couldn't help wonder if Wells had been younger, there might have been a chance for him to be signed to a professional contract after such a good season. Most Australians who sign as amateur free agents do so as teenagers and those in their early twenties are usually drafted playing college baseball in the US. During the early 1990s, when Wells was coming through the junior ranks, there was no academy on the Gold Coast, scouting in Australia wasn't customary and few Australians played college baseball. It's fair to say Wells had a tougher road to travel than young players of today.

Despite having players on his team who had past or current minor league baseball experience, Wells finished the season as the fourth-best batter on the team, with a .243 average and six doubles, which was equal second highest for Cavalry hitters.

His teammate, pitcher Phil Brassington, likewise accumulated service under the new and old ABL. It was pleasing to see them test their skills against a whole new generation of players. It seemed the past, present, and future had all united for the 2010/2011 season.

Each Blue Sox home series offered a chance to see new players and in addition the Blue Sox were firming as season favourites winning games with the best pitching staff in the league. It was pleasing my local team was doing so well, but I still felt connected to the past when the Sydney Blues were the Harbour City team. The 1995/1996 ABL Championship Series win by the Blues has a special place amongst all my baseball memories, as well as the players such as Gary White, Mark Shipley, Scott Tunkin, and Brendan Kingman. But this time around, I was older and needed to become familiar with the players on the Blue Sox team.

The Blue Sox had a good connection to the old ABL, with three players having participated in it. Chris Oxspring pitched for the Gold Coast Cougars during the 1997/1998 season; Craig Anderson pitched for the Hunter Eagles from 1996/1997 to 1997/1998 and the Sydney Storm during the 1998/1999 season; and Brendan Kingman was a utility and designated hitter on the Sydney Waves team from 1990/1991 to 1991/1992, Sydney Blues from 1992/1993 to 1996/1997, and Sydney Storm from 1997/1998 to 1998/1999.

Craig Anderson turned seventeen years old during his first ABL season in 1996/1997. He instantly displayed skills beyond his age by appearing in three games with an ERA of 2.61 over 10.1 innings pitched. Considering home run friendly Marathon Stadium was his home field, whilst at the Eagles he did especially well. Yet Anderson proved this was no fluke when he turned out for the Sydney Storm after the demise of the Eagles for the 1998/1999 season. He appeared in sixteen games with an ERA of 2.36 over 68.2 innings pitched. Anderson played minor league baseball within the Mariners and Orioles organisations from 1999–2008.

Anderson is one of a rare group of players to represent Australia in baseball at two Summer Olympic Games. He pitched in three games at Sydney 2000 and two at Athens 2004. Australia finished a disappointing seventh at Sydney 2000, but Anderson was the winning pitcher in the round-robin game against South Korea on September 18, 2000, which Australia won 5–3, and he pitched 4.1 innings. Dae-Sung Koo pitched 4.1 innings for South Korea in the same game. Unknown to Anderson at the time was the fact they would become Blue Sox teammates during the 2010/2011 ABL season. At Athens in 2004, he started Australia's first round-robin game against baseball powerhouse Cuba, where he pitched seven spirited innings and took the loss as Cuba won 4–1. But he was part of a team that surprised many opponents and took home the silver medal for baseball, which is one of Australia's greatest achievements in the sport to date.

Anderson finished the 2010/2011 ABL regular season with three wins and two losses and an ERA of 2.23 over 44.1 innings pitched.

Chris Oxspring was one of four players on the Sydney Blue Sox roster with Major League experience. He and Dae-Sung Koo played the whole season with the Blue Sox, and

Major Leaguers Trent Oeltjen and Richard Thompson also made appearances.

Oxspring is the epitome of a true-blue Aussie battler. It is important to emphasise that the term "battler" is applied in its purest definition, meaning a person who displays untiring valour under circumstances considered beyond their control. This in many ways is the fuel which drove his career to the lofty heights of an Olympic silver medal and playing Major League Baseball.

Oxspring's journey as a baseball player had no easy passes, as all his achievements came through grit and tremendous perseverance. His stint in the previous ABL was a polished five innings of pitching for the Gold Coast Cougars during the 1997/1998 season with a tidy ERA of 1.80 appearing in six games. He wasn't signed as a teenager and playing professionally at sixteen or seventeen years old, like many talented Australian players do today. His pathway to the top is one of the most admirable of any Aussie player I know of. At twenty-three years of age, he played independent baseball in the US with Cook County of the Frontier League. Whilst his travel to the Majors wasn't as long as American Chris "the thirty-three-year-old rookie" Coste, they both earned contracts with Major League organisations out of independent baseball. After posting an ERA of 3.10 over 29.0 innings pitched with Cook County during the 2000 season, he was signed as a free agent by the San Diego Padres on October 31, 2000.

He pitched within the Padres Organisation from 2001–2005. His numbers were respectable as a minor leaguer, yet in 2004 shares in Chris Oxspring soared during the Athens Olympic Games. He appeared in two games and was the winning pitcher in both. The first was against Italy, a round-robin game on August 17, 2004, where he pitched eight innings, giving up no runs. The final score was Australia six, Italy zero.

He was the starting pitcher in perhaps the best ever game played by Team Australia and that day he enshrined himself as a true battler. It was the semi-final game against Japan on August 24, 2004. Japan had an all-star team, with the outstanding Daisuke Matsuzaka pitching. Most people would have had Australia at long odds to win that game, but they didn't count on Chris Oxspring and Jeff Williams pitching Japan out of the contest. Slick fielding contained Japan's booming bats and a base hit by Brendan Kingman knocked in the winning run of the game. Oxspring pitched 6.2 innings for the win, and Australia went straight to the gold medal game by defeating Japan 1–0.

Oxspring's career continued to gain further momentum and on September 2, 2005, he made his Major League debut with the San Diego Padres, where he pitched in five games over twelve innings with an ERA of 3.75. He was released by the Padres on December 6, 2005 and spent 2006 pitching for the Hanshin Tigers in Japan's Nippon Professional Baseball Central League. After a season in Japan, the Milwaukee Brewers signed him as a free agent on December 15, 2006. He acknowledged the Brewers' then-pitching coach Mike Maddux as one of the best he ever received guidance from during the Brewers 2007 spring training. He was a reliable pitcher for AAA team Nashville, with seven wins and five losses and an ERA of 3.56 over 96.0 innings pitched. The Korean team, the LG Twins, bought out his contract and the Brewers released him on July 10, 2007, to play in the Korean Baseball Organization.

Oxspring spent the remainder of 2007 and all of 2008 pitching in Korea. Unfortunately in early 2009 and leading up to the World Baseball Classic, he suffered an injury to his pitching arm, which required surgery. He lost the entire 2009 season recovering and pitched in the Sydney Winter Baseball League in 2010 on his way back up.

Oxspring was the first starting pitcher in the new ABL pitching for the Sydney Blue Sox on November 6, 2010, when they played at Blue Town against the Canberra Cavalry. He was also the Blue Sox pitching coach. He pitched six innings, giving up just three hits, no runs and struck out eight batters. When the Blue Sox played the Melbourne Aces on December 10, 2010, he started the game and pitched 6.1 innings, conceding only five hits, no runs, and striking out eight. His ERA was just 0.67 and two days later on December 12 he was signed by the Detroit Tigers. The whole Australian baseball community was pleased when he signed because he had worked so hard to overcome his injury.

By the end of the regular ABL season, he had achieved four wins and two losses with an ERA of 2.23 over 68.2 innings pitched. He started 2011 with the Detroit Tigers AAA team Toledo, where he had difficulty with consistency. He appeared in eight games for one loss, and had an ERA of 6.53 over 20.2 innings pitched. The Tigers released him on May 24, 2011.

The independent team the Somerset Patriots of the Atlantic League picked up Oxspring for the remainder of 2011, where he teamed up with fellow Aussie and former Major Leaguer Justin Huber. Oxspring's numbers don't reflect the lack of run support he received as several of his losses were by one or two runs. He won five games and lost nine with an ERA of 4.17 over 105.2 innings pitched.

Oxspring formed a vital part of the deadliest pitching staff in the ABL during the 2010/2011 season. His Blue Sox teammate David Welch was awarded Pitcher of the Year, which was very impressive.

Dae-Sung Koo was the only foreign player on the Blue Sox roster during their first season. Yet he had chosen to make Sydney home, which meant the Blue Sox was the only team in the ABL that didn't have an imported player.

Koo's connection to Australia is much deeper than is often realised. He pitched in three games for South Korea at the Sydney 2000 Olympic Games and won a bronze medal. In many cultures, the family name is placed ahead of the first name and there can be variation when his name is translated, this is why his full name sometimes appears as Koo Dae-Sung and Gu Dae-Seong. For the 2000 Olympics, many records document him as Gu Dae-Seong.

Koo pitched against powerhouse Japan twice during Sydney 2000. The first occasion was the round-robin game on September 23, 2000, where he pitched six innings in a game South Korea won 7–6. He saved his absolute best for the final round bronze medal game against Japan by pitching all nine innings for the win. He struck out eleven batters and the final score was 3–1. Japan was favoured to win that game and South Korea had proved time and again they were very capable of beating their regional neighbours at various international fixtures. Given he pitched against Team Australia on September 18, a game Australia won 5–3, Australia finishing the 2000 Olympics ranked seventh was nowhere near their full capability.

Koo began his professional career in the Korean Baseball Organization with the Lotte Giants in 1993 and pitched for the Hanwha Eagles from 1994–2000. He clearly made quite an impression in Japan and played for the Orix Blue Wave in Japan's NPB Pacific League from 2001–2004. The only challenge which still lay in front of Koo was Major League Baseball, and on April 4, 2005, he made his Major League debut pitching for the New York Mets. He played his final MLB game on August 20, 2005. With the Mets, he pitched 23.0 innings in thirty-three games, his ERA was 3.91 with twenty-three strikeouts. As a National League team, he had two at-bats and collected a hit, which happened to be a double on May 21, 2005. The hit came off Randy "The Unit" Johnson, who was pitching for the New York Yankees at the time in an inter-league game.

A sacrifice bunt by Jose Reyes advanced Koo to third base, and Yankees catcher Jorge Posada concentrated on Reyes, with Koo slowing at third base, but he took off when he saw an opportunity at home plate as Posada had left it open. It was a close tag play after Posada received the ball from first base, but Koo was called safe at home and so he scored a run. Koo reportedly hadn't batted in a game in eighteen years. Subsequently, at the Major League level, he has a career .500 batting average and slugging of 1.000.

He then returned to Korea and pitched for the Hanwha Eagles from 2006–2010.

Koo made a significant impact in the ABL during the inaugural 2010/2011 season by winning the Reliever of the Year Award. He was a true lights-out man with an ERA of 1.00, appearing in eighteen games and pitching 27.0 innings, striking out thirty, and he was credited with two wins and one loss. At forty-one years old, he still had plenty left in his arm.

It was disappointing the Blue Sox didn't originally consider Brendan Kingman for a spot on the roster. There was a perception giving the younger players a chance was an important aspect to the ABL and at thirty-seven years old and overcoming an injury, Kingman had to wait most of the season for his chance.

It wasn't obvious initially the Blue Sox hitting was a bit weak, as they were well protected by good pitching. Yet by the end of the season, only two players with eighty or more at-bats batted over .300, they were Joshua Dean and Trent Schmutter.

Yet for me, history does count for something. In the previous ABL, Kingman was the Sydney Blues/Storm all-time home run leader with ninety-five. He ranks first and second for most in a season, hitting twenty-one in 1996/1997 for the Blues/Storm and twenty-seven in 1997/1998.

Kingman was one of the best right-handed Australian batters I've seen play. His ability to hit the ball with such crisp force and drive it to all parts of the field made him a deadly hitter. I actually pitched to him when I played for North Shore over the 2004/2005 summer. He was playing for the Canterbury Vikings at the time and never did I imagine I would have to try to strike out my favourite Aussie hitter. He slashed a single off me in one at-bat and flew out to centre field during the other. My pitch broke his bat on that occasion and I chased him into his dugout and begged for it as a souvenir, which he kindly gave me.

Kingman started his professional career with the Florida Marlins in 1992, where he stayed until 1995. He began in rookie ball and made it to high A ball with them. His minor league statistics during his time with the Marlins were decent, including eight home runs in 1995. The Marlins decided to release him and so he had to fight his way back into professional baseball.

It's fair to say he slugged his way back to the US, but it didn't come easy despite two solid seasons in the ABL from

1995/1996 to 1996/1997, where he had a batting average of .292 and .325.

In 1997/1998, Kingman smashed numerous ABL hitting records with his .487 average for the season, with twenty-seven home runs and a 1.083 slugging percentage. The Seattle Mariners signed him and his two-year hiatus from minor league baseball did him no harm.

Whilst playing on the Mariners high A ball team Lancaster in 1998, he produced a .340 season batting average with sixteen home runs. In 1999, he was promoted to the AA team New Haven, where he racked up a .279 batting average with ten home runs. Kingman made the right impression because he found himself on the Mariners' Major League forty-man roster for the 2000 season.

Kingman suffered an arm injury which hindered his 2000 season. He played eleven games with the Mariners AA team and another eleven games with the independent team the Catskill Cougars. It was a cruel end because Kingman had a Major League swing.

But Kingman continued on and proved his hitting skills were first class during the Athens 2004 Olympic Games with his consistent hitting. The high point was Australia's semi-final game against Japan.

Japan could taste a final-round gold medal game and all that stood in their way was Australia, a team they were expected to make easy work of in the semi-final. But they certainly didn't approach the game lightly, with Daisuke Matsuzaka as their starting pitcher. He was an eighteen-year-old when he made his debut with the Seibu Lions in Japan's NPB Pacific League on April 7, 1999. From 1999–2006, he was a pitching sensation, amassing numerous season records and noted for his excellent fielding. He was also playing in his second Olympic Games, having participated in Sydney 2000. He pitched ten innings in Japan's 4–2 loss to Team USA on September 17, 2000. His first game of the 2004 Olympics was against Cuba, where he threw 8.1 innings for a 6–3 win in their round-robin game on August 17, 2004. Japan was clearly unleashing its best hurler on Team Australia. It nearly paid off for them as Matsuzaka struck out thirteen Australian batters in 7.2 innings. But Brendan Kingman cracked one of the most memorable hits of his career when he lined a Matsuzaka pitch into right field, driving in the only run of the game. He had hit safely against one of the world's most talented pitchers, which was all the proof needed to confirm he had a Major League swing.

Matsuzaka cemented his talent in the US when he joined the Boston Red Sox for the 2007 MLB season. He made his Red Sox Major League debut on April 5, 2007 and had a decent season with fifteen wins and twelve losses, an ERA of 4.40, and 201 strikeouts. But his first Major League season was brilliantly capped off with a World Series championship. His 2008 season was probably his best with eighteen wins and three losses, an ERA of 2.90, and 154 strikeouts. He has had a glittering career and Brendan Kingman has recorded a base hit off him!

Seeing Kingman back in the ABL brought back a lot of good memories. He proved he should have been on the Blue Sox team the entire 2010/2011 season as his batting average was .455 in four regular season games. His slugging average was 1.091, and he hit two home runs. I'm glad my favourite hitter is in a rare group of players to have participated in both versions of the ABL.

The Blue Sox delivered on showcasing current Major Leaguers as Trent Oeltjen, who had spent part of the 2010

MLB season with the Los Angeles Dodgers, appeared in two games and Richard Thompson, who spent a long portion of the 2010 MLB season with the Los Angeles Anaheim Angels, made three pitching appearances. Both Oeltjen and Thompson were on the Athens 2004 Olympic silver medal team with Oxspring and Kingman. Thompson was also the youngest player on the Athens team at twenty years and forty-six days old.

I caught up with Thompson while he was pitching for the Blue Sox, and he thanked me for giving his former Angels teammate Sean O'Sullivan a pair of Aussie flag board shorts while in Kansas City. "He sent me a text message and he loves the board shorts," Thompson said. Perhaps always curious for exact details, I asked him, "Do the shorts fit him okay?" He replied with a nod of his head and smiled, "As far as I know they do."

It was a triumph for the ABL and the Blue Sox that Oeltjen and Thompson participated, as showcasing Australia's best talent was vital for new and existing fans of the game.

When the Brisbane Bandits played the Blue Sox in Sydney on November 27, the opportunity to shake hands with Australia's most successful former Major League player, David Nilsson, brought back more memories of the previous ABL and his illustrious career. Nilsson had the ability to take teams to another level with his potent bat and extensive experience. As a Sydney Blues fan, Nilsson could break hearts with a single swing, and so it was a lot easier to support him when he was in the US playing MLB for the Milwaukee Brewers or when he took the field for Team Australia. In the new ABL, he was the Bandits' first field manager.

He played his whole Major League career with the Brewers, making his debut on May 18, 1992, and playing his final game on October 3, 1999. He was the first of four Australians to have played for the Brewers to date, followed by Graeme Lloyd, Trent Durrington, and Grant Balfour.

Nilsson was a true baseball trailblazer for Australia, and he is so far the only Aussie all-star. He is frequently regarded as the best catcher in Brewers' history. Often people within Australian baseball circles wonder who the next Dave Nilsson will be, however the question should always take into consideration the factors which made him the player he was. He hit 105 home runs during his MLB career and had two seasons where he hit twenty or more home runs. Considering he mostly played as a catcher and had a career .284 batting average is further proof of his special talent.

Yet Nilsson's pedigree can be attributed somewhat to his nature and nurture. To begin with, he came from an Aussie baseball family. His older brothers Bob and Gary both played professionally in the US. Standing at 1.92 metres tall and weighing between 83–90 kilograms during his playing days, Dave had the physique of a high-performance athlete. When you combine Dave's family influence and his physical attributes, this set the foundation for a talented player.

It is important to remember Australian athletes with similar physical attributes often choose other sports ahead of baseball. Cricket, rugby league, rugby union, and Australian rules football are the sporting pathways many athletes take in Australia. So with baseball behind these sports in terms of participation, it was lucky to secure an athlete of Dave's prowess.

The question of who will be the next Dave Nilsson is difficult to answer. This is in part due to the fact it is rare in Australia to have a family with such a strong disposition toward baseball. Also, through years of hard work, Nilsson established himself as a genuine power hitter and whilst Luke Hughes and Trent Oeltjen are working to prove themselves as capable Major League hitters, Nilsson reached a higher echelon than any other Aussie player has to date.

With the return of the ABL and a continuous flow of Aussies in professional baseball leagues overseas, there is certainly potential for another player of Nilsson's calibre to emerge. I predict such a talent can only come once every twenty or so years, as baseball in Australia is in the shadow of so many other sports—but its capacity to grow is certainly encouraging.

I had with me for the Blue Sox versus Bandits series my *Sydney 2000—The Games of the XXVII Olympiad—The official Souvenir Book—Gold Collector Series.* The book features Olympic baseball from pages 104–111. There is a picture of Nilsson batting on page 110 and I hoped to have him sign it for me.

Nilsson's MLB career is decorated with numerous historical achievements for Australian baseball. One of my favourites is as a catcher he created the first all-Aussie battery (pitcher and catcher combination) when he caught for Australian Brewers teammate Graeme Lloyd on April 14, 1993. Despite his many accomplishments and chance to continue to earn millions after the 1999 season, he chose to play for the Chunichi Dragons in Japan's NPB Central League. This enabled him to participate in the Sydney Olympic Games.

Having won the gold medal at the 1999 Baseball Intercontinental Cup, which was held in Sydney, and serving as a cornerstone of the team Nilsson did his absolute best for Team Australia, he played catcher and designated hitter between September 17, 2000, and September 24, 2000, with an incredible batting average of .565 but his contribution couldn't prevent Australia from finishing seventh.

The great Australian sporting dream to medal at the Olympic Games was deeply embedded in Nilsson's heart and mind as he returned to professional baseball in the US, playing sixteen games for the Atlanta Braves AAA team Richmond during the 2004 season.

At the Athens 2004 Olympic Games, he played all his games from August 15–August 25 as a catcher and provided tremendous experience and leadership. The fact Australia took home the silver medal was a nice reward for the team and Nilsson. However this Olympic baseball achievement isn't well known amongst the general sporting public in Australia. Nilsson didn't hang up his cleats by any means as he represented Australia at the first World Baseball Classic in 2006.

The last time I had met him in person was on February 13, 1999, when he attended the Sydney Storm and Gold Coast Cougars second ABL Championship Series Game as an official rather than a player. The Cougars won. Amongst the disappointment of Sydney losing he cheered me right up when he signed a ball for me. I was nineteen years old, and I had received my first Dave Nilsson autograph—it was a moment I'll never forget.

There I was at thirty-one years old, with so many great memories of Nilsson. I got to meet him again on the night of November 27. He walked a metre past the dugout exit door to a line of people, from kids to adults, requesting autographs from him. As I stood there it was fantastic to see he was so well remembered and appreciated. He put down his bag and signed away until every request was satisfied.

I ambled toward him and said, “Hello, Dave,” as he gave me his full attention I asked, “Could you please sign my Sydney 2000 Olympic book for me?”

He replied with warmth, “I'd love to.” I knew there might not be another opportunity apart from that series in Sydney to speak with him so I took the opportunity to say “I've written a couple of Aussie baseball books. I have one called *Boomerang Baseball* and you're mentioned quite a few times.”

“I've heard of that book, I saw something on the ABF or Queensland Baseball website, which had some details about it.”

“I'd be happy to organise some copies for you.”

“That would be much appreciated.” Four Nilsson brothers played in the former ABL, and his parents were also loyally involved with the game.

“How about I send five copies to you care of the Brisbane Bandits front office?”

“That would be great, thank you.” He had to leave as the team bus was about to depart, but it was nice to shake his hand for a second time. Every experience I've had with Dave Nilsson has been positive. People often don't realise all the work he did in the previous ABL as a player and even an administrator was for free. His involvement in the new ABL is a credit to his ongoing dedication to the sport in Australia.

One interesting aspect of the ABL is not realising you could be watching a future star. The Bandits started Ryan Searle on the mound for the game on November 27. He took the loss, completing five innings. Not knowing a lot about Searle, it wasn't until I reviewed his minor league statistics with the Cubs organisation it clicked he could maybe become the first Aussie to play MLB with them.

At twenty-one years old, he had spent part of the 2010 minor league season pitching for the Cubs high A ball team, Daytona. There he had accumulated an ERA of 4.60 over 15.2 innings of work. He started 2011 with Daytona, and his ERA was 1.59 over 28.1 innings. He found himself with the AA team Tennessee, where he would spend the bulk of his season. His ERA of 3.51 over 84.2 innings showed he belonged there.

Often a player becomes distinguished to a fan of baseball by one performance which captures their attention. For me it was when Searle pitched 7.1 innings for Team Australia at the 2011 Baseball World Cup in the second round game on October 11, 2011, against Canada, a game Australia won 7–0. Searle was the winning pitcher, and he only gave up three hits and one walk and struck out six. On November 27, 2010, if I had only known what the next year contained for Searle, I would have asked for an autograph when I had the chance.

The Melbourne Aces came to Sydney for a series which included the weekend of December 4–5, a cause of excitement for me. Melbourne is a decent hotbed for Aussie baseball talent and the Aces' roster included players with Major League experience, such as hitter and utility fielder, Justin Huber and pitcher Travis Blackley. Blackley was a Major Leaguer with the Mariners at just twenty-one years old during the 2004 MLB season and also pitched for the Giants in 2007. I had not seen either Huber or Blackley play on home soil. The most I had observed of them overseas was brief television footage. Having followed both their careers for over five years led to much anticipation and was another gift of the ABL as the league gave them an opportunity to play at home during the US winter.

During the same Aces series, I had become acquainted with Jason Horne, a favourite Aussie fan of the Kansas City Royals. It wasn't as though I had to look hard to find him. I saw a spectator with a Royals cap and jersey with "Horne" and the number one written on the back collecting food from one of the vendors at the grandstand, and walked up and introduced myself.

"Hey, dude, it's good to meet you at last," was his reply. I'm always reminded how baseball has introduced me to plenty of new friends. To have had international conversations regarding Jason and finally meeting him in person was all thanks to the ABL giving fans a local product to enjoy.

"Justin Huber is on the roster for Aces. We should try and meet him while he is here," I suggested.

"Sounds great."

I had also come to know Sydney Blue Sox American intern Alexis Busch. I've had times in my life where I ate, lived, and slept baseball, but Alexis had energy and passion for the sport which soared high above the sky. She played women's baseball in Sydney determinedly and loved all facets of the game. She was the San Francisco Giants first-ever bat girl, and greeted Barry Bonds at home plate with congratulations after he hit his five hundredth home run on April 17, 2001—an image I remember seeing on television. She had come to Sydney with her boyfriend Nick Vos, who was spending the summer sailing with local yacht clubs. As a Giants fan, I told Alexis the Aces roster included Travis Blackley, who had pitched for the Giants in 2007 and the series would probably present an opportunity to meet him. She smiled and said, "Sure."

Whilst it would have been possible to meet the players after each game, I caught a break after speaking with Peter

Dihm, who was Baseball Victoria's chairman for twenty years. He was accompanying the team. Rain had caused game delays over the weekend, but it gave me a great opportunity to talk with Peter at length. He was beaming having the ABL back and with Melbourne in the hunt for the championship. I agreed their roster was impressive. Peter struck me as a loyal baseball advocate who had given tens of thousands of hours to the sport in mainly Victoria and around Australia.

His friendly demeanour certainly made my day when he first introduced Jason Horne and I to Justin Huber during one of the rain delays. Jason had actually left a note in Justin's locker at the Royals during a visit wishing him well. I asked him to sign an autograph for Jason, which he did. The two seemed to talk like old friends about the Royals. I gave Justin a copy of each of my baseball books and told him the Royals fondly remember him. Jason and I received exciting news from him! He had signed with the Minnesota Twins for 2011, where he had played his last MLB game on September 11, 2009. He spent the 2010 season in Japan.

During yet another rain delay, Peter introduced Alexis and I to Travis Blackley. Alexis was a bit pressed for time as she had things to see to around the venue, but spoke with Blackley for a few minutes. Barry Bonds came into the conversation and Travis told her how he asked Bonds to sign a ball for his wife and one for her mother, which he happily did, but Bonds told Blackley not to give up any early home runs as he did in his first Giants pitching start. This wasn't said in a condescending tone but rather Bonds didn't want the opposition to get the jump on Blackley, who at that point had participated in seven MLB games, with one more to follow with the Giants in 2007, bringing his total to eight at that stage of his career. Interestingly, during that season he had three at-bats where he collected a base hit, giving him a .333 average.

Alexis was pleased to meet the second Aussie San Francisco Giant—the first was Damian Moss—and they shook hands and she wished Blackley well.

I'm always reminded to never take anything for granted and it came as a complete shock to me when I learnt Alexis was lost at sea and presumed deceased on April 14, 2012, in a sailing accident off the coast of San Francisco. A year and a few months prior, she was in Australia helping the ABL, which made it so difficult to fathom, and my deepest condolences go out to Nick and her family and friends.

She would be pleased Blackley signed with the San Francisco Giants for the 2012 MLB season, where he earned a recall to the Majors.

When I met Blackley on the same day as Alexis, he instantly recognised me. "Hey, I got your book in the mail in the US. Nice work, but there was no letter with it?" The book he was referring to was *The American Dream: From Perth to Sacramento*.

"I thought if I sent it to your Oakland Athletics AAA team with a letter they might think it was fan mail, whereas if the book was posted straight from my publisher it might be considered official mail for you."

"I received it fine, and it's good." Blackley was a colourful personality with an extensive collection of tattoos on his arms. He spoke with me like I wasn't a stranger. Rather, I felt we were old high school classmates, even though we're three years apart in age and went to schools in different Australian cities and states. I talked with him for quite a while. His career, which has included stints with the Mariners, Giants, Phillies, Diamondbacks, Mets, and Athletics organisations, has made his baseball journey well-travelled. He also spent some time playing in Mexico.

"I've signed to play with the KIA Tigers in Korea for this season." He said, "It's going to be nice to have the stability of not having the team changes which can sometimes happen during a minor league season. There I can just focus on getting to know my teammates and working to help the club win." One facet of professional baseball which isn't fully realised is the fallout when Major League clubs make roster changes. It can have a cascading impact, as the priorities of the team rosters down the line can change, putting some players to work and leaving others out altogether. The Korean Baseball Organization doesn't have a multileveled minor league system like the US, so there isn't the movement which comes with it.

I gave Blackley a copy of *Boomerang Baseball.* Again it was fantastic to meet a player I had known for years through Internet articles, playing statistics and the occasional piece of television footage. As a left-handed pitcher with Big League experience, it seemed plenty of doors would be open for him and I was thrilled when he made it back with the Giants in 2012.

I went home on December 5 feeling very satisfied even though the game ended in a 1–1 draw between the Blue Sox and Aces. By the end of the regular season, the Blue Sox finished first by half a game so that afternoon against the Aces was a lot more than a draw.

The Blue Sox were away, playing the Adelaide Bite starting from December 16. I decided I would drive down to Canberra, as I had some time available to watch the Cavalry play the Perth Heat at Narrabundah Ballpark. I drove down and back on both the sixteenth and the seventeenth.

Whilst Blacktown Olympic Park in Sydney was built for baseball, it lacks any glaring indicators of being an Australian venue. Apart from some Aussie flags, there is little about the diamonds that scream Australia. This is partially due to how barren the three fields are, with trees basically skirting the facility.

Narrabundah Ballpark looks, smells, and sounds Australian. Its pleasant eucalyptus gum trees exudes summer sap and *Acacia pravissima* (oven's wattle) drifts through the air with the afternoon breeze and creates small clouds of bright yellow blooms. The kookaburras' laughing call from the branches of trees made me feel at home. All I needed was my favourite bird, the rainbow lorikeet, an Australasian parrot and it would have been the perfect-picture Australian baseball backdrop.

The kookaburra is a close second favourite. As a carnivorous bird, they hunt with plenty of audacity and aren't afraid to make a meal of a snake or a lizard. Their large triangular bill is sharp and tough, which makes easy work of dicing and serving up their tucker. A kookaburra is distinctive not just by its personality, but its look is quite unique. They are usually brown and white in colour, with a large head, brown eyes, and a stocky bird of nearly half a metre wingspan when fully grown.

The rainbow lorikeet is different to the kookaburra in so many ways with its high-pitched call and a body size of about thirty centimetres as adults. Many have a deep blue coloured head with a light red hooked beak, a greenish-yellow nuchal collar, some blue across their chests, mostly green wings, and their backs and tails include some light red and yellow.

As a boy growing up in the Sydney suburbs of East Lindfield, Pymble, Wahroonga, and Hornsby, kookaburras and rainbow lorikeets were a familiar sight.

The combination of nature's beauty and the sea of Canberra Cavalry bright orange lining the ballpark's fences and various amenities ignited a vibrant energy all through the place.

I arrived several hours before the 7:00 p.m. start time. It was fantastic to see the teams warm up and gave me a good opportunity to interact with players from both teams, as there were a few breaks between fielding drills and batting practice.

I was pleasantly surprised Perth Heat players Allan de San Miguel, Tim Kennelly, and Mathew Kennelly all recognised me. I had sent them and other West Australian players copies of *The American Dream: From Perth to Sacramento* during their most recent minor league season in the US. My picture is on the back cover, making it hard to miss this baseball fanatic.

Whilst there are several talented Australian catchers playing professionally in the US, it seems West Australia has developed an assembly line for producing backstops, as de San Miguel and the Kennelly brothers are among the best in the country.

We talked for a while near the visiting team dugout as Perth waited for Canberra to finish their fielding work. Tim Kennelly mentioned, "You've covered life in the minors for an Aussie well."

De San Miguel said with an encouraging tone, "Keep more of those books coming."

As Tim and Mathew Kennelly both play for different organisations, I asked Mathew if they'd ever come up against each other in the minor leagues. "No, we've been in different leagues despite playing at the same level." Tim had been with the Phillies organisation since 2005, playing as high as AA, and Mathew, who is the younger, had been with the Braves organisation from 2007 and as of 2010 had reached high A ball.

They both made history as brothers appearing for Team Australia during the Baseball World Cup in 2009. On September 9, 2009, they played against the Czech Republic in beautiful Prague. Australia won the game 17–4, and Tim smacked two home runs in his first two at-bats and Mathew hit two doubles.

The Heat's extensive catching wealth included de San Miguel, who played within the Twins organisation from 2005 and as high as AAA in 2009 and 2010.

When the Cavalry finished their work on the field, they went into their clubhouse for a short while. I walked over and stood nearby while some players took swings in the batting cage, others used the time to have a bit of a break. Michael Collins spotted me on his way to the cages and said with a friendly smile, "Hey, good to see you down here."

Teenager Robbie Perkins was there as a bullpen catcher and had a few bats in his hands to take to the players at the cages. He must have lost his grip on one as he walked past me, as it swung very close to my groin. I jumped backward a little and said, "Watch the nuts, kid!" I think he thought I was being serious, and he replied, "Sorry." I smiled and laughed to let him know I wasn't angry. In 2012, Robbie signed with the Colorado Rockies. His older brother Kyle spent some time playing minor league baseball with the New York Yankees and he was one of the Cavalry's catchers playing behind Michael Collins and South Korean import Sung-Woo Jang. When the Yankees released Kyle in 2011 he turned his attention toward pitching.

The Cavalry had some notable international talent. Two who particularly stood out were Dutchman Mariekson "Didi" Gregorius and American-born German Donald Lutz. Gregorius was a shortstop and Lutz an outfielder and they were both imports from the Cincinnati Reds organisation.

Gregorius as a shortstop was measurable against the best one I've seen to date in Australia, that being Mark Shipley. I only saw his older brother, Major Leaguer Craig, play a few times on taped games, but I saw Mark play dozens of times for the Sydney Blues/Storm. He had the agility of an acrobat, the deft hands of a surgeon and a glove which didn't know the meaning of the word error. His arm snapped freakish throws regardless of whether he had both feet on the ground or which way his balance was leaning toward. He won a record three ABL Gold Gloves for his skill in the previous league.

I would have liked a chat with Gregorius, but he seemed like a quiet fellow, comfortable around his teammates with good eye contact and a few smiles. His fielding had caught my attention in Sydney, with his ability to spring to his left and right with lightning speed glove the ball with a swift precise scoop, and fire the ball with a rocket blast. It was clear Gregorius was the best shortstop I had seen since Shipley. The ABL saw fit to award him the season Gold Glove for fielding excellence. Gregorius recorded a .189 season batting average with one home run and he played a team-high thirty-six games. If hitting was an area he needed to improve, he certainly did during the 2011 minor league season by recording a .289 batting average split between high A ball and AA with seven home runs.

Gregorius's Australian connection didn't end with the 2010/2011 ABL season. He played for the Netherlands at the 2011 Baseball World Cup in Panama and Team Australia faced the Dutch on October 12, finishing the game on October 13 due to rain delays with the Dutch eventually winning 2–1. The Netherlands defeated Cuba 2–1 in the final on October 15 to win their first title. Gregorius made his Major League debut with the Reds on September 5, 2012, and it was pleasing to see him first in the ABL.

Donald Lutz was also on the inaugural Cavalry team and what an athlete! Built like a hard-running rugby union back rower, he was someone you wanted on your team. Born in Watertown, New York, his family returned to Germany when he was still an infant. Despite his imposing physique his cheerful grin radiated a gracious personality.

When he saw me standing there watching the team go through its paces, he said, "Hey, how you doing?" It was pleasing he was interested, as some athletes can be known for being in their own world. Not Lutz, though...he stopped and gave me his full attention.

"I'm well, how are you enjoying your time in the ABL?"

"I'm seeing some good pitches and I feel like I'm going to go into spring training with something extra." He fielded either in the outfield or played first base, but proved he was a slugger from head to toe by cranking out a triple on December 16 off Heat ace pitcher Liam Hendriks, who within a year was playing Major League ball with the Minnesota Twins.

On December 16, Lutz pounded the biggest home run I've seen to date in the new ABL off Perth pitcher Tyler Anderson in the sixth inning. It sailed over the right field fence, I estimate it would have gone 120–140 metres as it flew so far over the fence it was a speck when I last saw it. Lutz was quoted in the *Canberra Times* as saying, "I got the pitch I was looking for." What a scary thought if you're a pitcher, knowing Lutz might find the pitch he wants and dispatch it hundreds of metres from home plate.

Interestingly, Lutz didn't start playing baseball until he was in his mid-teens, yet he has natural talent, and has also enhanced his skills further with hard work.

For the two games I attended in Canberra, the Cavalry defeated the Perth Heat on December 16, 7–5, and on December 17, 9–5.

Lutz had a season batting average of .260 with the Cavalry, and he lead the team in triples with three, home runs by crushing five, twenty-one runs batted in and slugging with a mark of .520.

His connection to the Canberra Cavalry didn't end after the ABL season. When Australia played Germany at the 2011 Baseball World Cup, on October 9, 2011 Lutz hit a monster home run off his former Cavalry teammate Hayden Beard, and needless to say he got the pitch he was looking for! Australia won that game, 9–6.

Having spent the off-season playing in the ABL, Lutz's predication he would go into spring training with something extra proved to be correct. Call it German precision and engineering or a breakout season playing with the Reds A ball team, but Lutz posted a .301 batting average and a whopping twenty home runs for his 2011 minor league season.

The ABL claim as showcasing the best local and rising international baseball talent continued to be evident at each series I attended.

Liam Hendriks was the starting pitcher for the Perth Heat on December 16, the first time I had seen him pitch live. He was signed by the Minnesota Twins as an amateur free agent on February 25, 2007, and he immediately showed his class on the mound by posting a 2.05 ERA as an eighteen-year-old playing for the Twins Gulf League rookie team during the 2007 minor league season.

My connection to Hendriks is very unique as his mother was one of the first people in Australia to purchase a copy of, *The American Dream: From Perth to Sacramento*, in 2009. I didn't know this straight away, as I couldn't see who purchased my books. I could only see the date, quantity, and the seller in sales reports. It came to my attention when she e-mailed Peter Flintoff, who together with Adrian Dunn, form the writer/editor team of the *Flintoff and Dunn's Australian Major League Baseball* website and publications. I had named a fictional Australian Baseball League in my novel *The Flintoff and Dunn Shield*.

Liam's mother brought this to their attention, and was also pleased many locations in Perth, which are part of the narrative, are areas she and the Hendriks family were familiar with.

Attention to detail was clearly a gift she passed on to her son Liam because in 2010 he posted a combined ERA of 1.74 playing A ball and high A, over 108.2 innings with 105 strikeouts and only conceding twelve walks. A mind that can absorb and put into action the finest details and implement coaching advice to expand the precision of their natural game is the mental facet of baseball Hendriks appears to have a firm hold of.

Hendriks's talent is confirmed by the fact in 2010 he reached the Twins high A ball team and spent the bulk of his season there, but within a year he went from there to AA, AAA, and the Majors. He made his Major League debut for the Twins on September 6, 2011, at just twenty-two years old.

The first time I saw any footage of Hendriks pitching was from the 2009 Baseball World Cup, yet again the ABL gave me a chance to see an Australian talent in action on home soil.

After the game on December 16, I spoke with Hendriks. He recognised me from my author photograph. I had also sent him a copy of *The American Dream: From Perth to Sacramento* while he was in the US. "I already had a copy as my mum sent me hers, but thank you for thinking of me."

"Your mum e-mailed Peter Flintoff regarding the reference in there to *The Flintoff and Dunn Shield*; she must be good with details."

"Yeah, she is. Nothing gets past her," he said proudly.

If I had known what the next year would contain for Hendriks, I would have asked for an autograph when I had the chance.

My time in Canberra was pleasantly stacked with opportunities to meet and talk with players.

With a six-team competition, four teams go through to the postseason. First and second play a major semi-final, over three games, with the winner going straight into the ABL championship series then a best-of-three minor semi-final series between third and fourth with the loser bowing out and the winner playing the loser of the major semi-final in a three-game series for a place in the Championship Series.

The 2010/2011 ABL season came down to the wire, with Brisbane and Canberra still a mathematical chance of going to the postseason—if some other league results went their way—but with a few weeks to go, they both still had a shot at it. The regular season finished with Sydney in first with twenty-four wins and fifteen losses, followed by Perth, Adelaide, Melbourne, Brisbane, and Canberra in sixth with twelve wins and twenty-four losses.

I attended the major semi-final series in Sydney against the Perth Heat, which went from January 27–28, 2011. The Heat didn't hesitate in bringing out their big guns, with Major League infielder Luke Hughes and AAA pitcher Brendan Wise. Both players had appeared during the regular ABL season at various times, with Hughes participating in twenty-three games and recording a batting average of .337 and knocking out five home runs. Wise pitched 4.1 innings over four games and didn't give up a hit or a run.

The Heat won the first game 4–2 and had seven hits to the Blue Sox's four. In game two, the Heat went straight to a home championship series by defeating the Blue Sox 6–0.

I spoke with Luke Hughes on January 27, 2011. When he had a short break after batting practice, he came back to the main grandstand to grab a drink. "Well done on hitting a home run for your first Major League hit."

"Thank you."

"I named a character in *The American Dream: From Perth to Sacramento* after you and Damian Moss. The lead protagonist is a Perth guy named Damian Hughes."

"Thanks." He sounded a bit surprised. I had sent him a copy, but he had spent a fair portion of the 2010 US season injured, which meant his whereabouts were quite mobile as he rehabbed. It was likely the book went astray.

I told him in a reasonably serious tone, "You know, you make it difficult for me when I'm in America." The smile slipped from Hughes's face, and he appeared puzzled. I continued, "Oh, don't give me that, all the pretty ladies over there expect every Aussie to look like you with blue eyes, blonde hair, and a bit of a tan. If you're not a surfy looking hunk, all that's left to work with is the Australian accent, which didn't win any hearts for me a few months back."

Hughes laughed for a moment and then replied, "I'm sorry you're finding it tough going over there, just keep trying."

I spoke with Brendan Wise after the game on January 27, 2011 in which he recorded a pitching save. He had exited from the dugout field access way and was walking under the grandstand when I walked up to him. "Congratulations on a fantastic 2010 season. You deserved to be called up to the Majors," I said.

He humbly smiled and said, "Thank you." He spent most of the year with Detroit's AAA team, Toledo. He posted an ERA of 2.08 over fifty-two innings of work.

"I sent you a copy of *The American Dream: From Perth to Sacramento* did you receive it?"

"Yes, I did, but I haven't met you before and there was no note with it."

"I figured it might reach you easier that way."

"It did, thank you for thinking of me."

To be able to have seen Wise and Hughes play on home soil and meet them was yet another bonus.

After the Adelaide Bite defeated the Melbourne Aces two games to zip in the minor semi-final, the Blue Sox had one last crack at going through to the championship series, playing at home again, where the preliminary final series took place from February 4–6, 2011.

The Adelaide Bite was a solid hitting team with not quite as much punch as the Perth Heat. Yet on February 4, 2011, one of the greatest individual pitching achievements occurred in either version of the ABL. Sydney pitching ace David Welch threw a no-hitter! Sydney won the game 8–0, and Welch made history as he pitched the first no-hitter in the new ABL and the only nine inning complete game no-no in either ABL, which included ten strikeouts. It was a wonderful achievement for the sport in Australia and for Welch.

Despite Sydney making a great start by winning game one, they lost game two 4–0, and Adelaide booked its spot in the championship series by taking game three in a marathon fifteen-inning game, 7–4.

The preliminary final series gave me a chance to see several players on the Adelaide team in action. For years, I had kept track of Adrian Burnside's career as a pitcher, and he is quite a unique story. Born in Alice Springs in Australia's Northern Territory, he instantly became a trailblazer when he signed with the Los Angeles Dodgers. He pitched in the previous ABL for the Adelaide Giants for three seasons between 1996/1997 and 1998/1999. Mainly used as a reliever, he appeared in fourteen games during the 1998/1999 season and he recorded an ERA of 3.52 over 38.1 innings pitched. He played minor league baseball for five organisations, which included the Los Angeles Dodgers, Pittsburgh Pirates, Detroit Tigers, Toronto Blue Jays, and San Diego Padres. He reached every level in the US except the Major Leagues, and in 2005 whilst pitching for Toronto's AAA team Syracuse, I felt he was a bit unlucky, especially as a left-handed pitcher, to not get a shot at the Majors with an ERA of 2.98 over 57.1 innings pitched.

He is certainly well travelled, having pitched for the Yomiuri Giants in Japan's NPB Central League in 2008 and the Nexen Heroes in the Korean Baseball Organization during the 2010 season. He also pitched on Australia's 2004 Olympic silver medal team during the round-robin phase and on August 22, 2004, he pitched four innings against Canada.

To be on home soil and have a chance to see Burnside pitch was another wonderful perk of the new ABL. He played part of the season and his regular season ABL statistics for 2010/2011 was an ERA of 3.72 over 9.2 innings pitched.

As he resides in San Diego, California, his Australian family cherish opportunities to see him take the mound. They travelled from South Australia to watch the Sydney preliminary final series. I took a moment to talk with his dad after game two and said, "I've been waiting a long time to see your son play in Australia." In the marathon game three on February 6, 2011, he pitched 2.2 innings and gave up no runs.

"We look forward to seeing him play whenever we can," his dad said. There's nothing better than seeing proud parents at baseball games and the Burnsides have so many reasons to be pleased with Adrian.

I had sent copies of both my books to Adrian, and whilst he talked with his family after game two by the first base side of the spectator fence, I waited for an opportunity to talk with him. His dad made it easy by looking in my direction and saying, "This fellow has been waiting a long time to see you pitch." Adrian came over and shook my hand. I knew I might not get another opportunity anytime soon so I asked him, "Did you receive a copy of the Aussie baseball–themed books I sent in the mail?"

"Yes, I did, thank you," he said, smiling gratefully. He continued, "I've read the one about the Australian that goes over to the US, and it's pretty good work." It's a lot of effort trying to get somewhere writing books, but feedback from a seasoned professional player like Burnside means a lot.

Then, Adelaide Bite infielder and minor leaguer Stefan Welch noticed me standing there and might have overhead Burnside discussing the books. "You're that guy who wrote that book? You sent me a copy too." Welch had played in the minors with the Mets from 2007.

"Yes, that's me. What did you think of it?" I asked.

"I loved it. My girlfriend read it first, but the whole concept of it with those themed-based chapters was great."

"Thank you so much for the wonderful feedback. How about I send you a copy of my latest book when your minor league season starts?"

"Sure that sounds great, thank you." I posted him a copy of *Boomerang Baseball* care of the Mets high A ball team, St. Lucie.

Up until 2010, the highest number of home runs Welch hit in a single season of minor league baseball was eight, but in 2011 whilst playing again for St. Lucie, he hit sixteen home runs. He also increased his 2010 batting average of .256 to .271. I'm sure there are a number of factors which contributed to Welch's hitting statistics rising, part of me feels appearing in forty ABL games for 2010/2011 and having 154 at-bats may have contributed to him going into spring training and the 2011 season in peak condition. He was yet another Australian player I kept track of in the minor leagues and finally got to see play.

Adelaide had plenty of hitting talent on their roster and three of the top ten ABL hitters for the 2010/2011 season were Bite players, including Americans James McOwen and Quincy Latimore and Australian 2004 Olympic silver medallist Tom Brice.

The 2010/2011 ABL Championship Series went to three games, with Adelaide winning game one 4–3, Perth taking game two 9–2 and the Heat becoming the first champions of the new ABL when they won game three 7–1.

Baseball was certainly back, and it was very satisfying to see so many games and talented players on home soil.

Within a few weeks of the ABL season ending, my mind was made up: I would visit the US again. The idea of seeing some more MLB games over there, and spending time with my mate Chris Vaccaro, was plenty to look forward to. My expectations were to enjoy another holiday in America, yet the events that transpired completely exceeded what I had in mind.

CHAPTER 6
THE NEW YORK YANKEES

I booked my trip to the US using Qantas Frequent Flyer points, but Mother Nature unleashed a series of natural disasters, which resulted in plenty of travel difficulty.

It began on March 11, 2011 when the Tohoku earthquake and tsunami struck Japan, devastating numerous coastal cities and causing massive destruction to the city of Sendai. The loss of life and damage was a grim reminder of how powerful nature can be. If this wasn't enough to worry about, the Fukushima Daiichi Nuclear Power Plant meltdown left the world breathless, but thankfully further catastrophe was averted.

On May 21, there was the Grimsvotn volcanic eruption in Iceland and ash from the volcano caused flight delays across Europe. I became concerned the ash could progress to North America and stop me from travelling, but luckily it didn't.

Whoever said things happen in threes was totally right because on June 4 the Puyehue-Cordon Caulle volcanic eruption occurred in Chile and brought most air traffic to a standstill in the Southern Hemisphere.

I had a lot to feel anxious about. To begin with, using frequent flyer points can mean taking the long way somewhere and that's exactly how it worked out for me. On June 23, I was scheduled to fly from Sydney to Tokyo and then Tokyo to New York. I waited nervously for news that permitted international flights from Australia, and it was only about a week before my departure date the all-clear was given.

The next hurdle was Japan, as it was suggested going there may present some risks given the nuclear power plant meltdown. It wasn't an official travel warning, yet it certainly gave me something to think about. My parents were concerned, but I decided nothing was going to stop me.

Qantas was grateful for passenger loyalty in spite of all the events and issued me free tickets to their international frequent flyer lounge. With all the apprehension leading up to the trip, I must admit it was a nice touch by Qantas. I had a night flight, and sitting in the lounge area with an amazing view of the tarmac, all the lights, taxiing planes and even some of the Sydney skyline was a wonderful way to begin a holiday. It was peaceful too, away from the hustle and bustle of standard commuting. I had use of a desktop computer, comfortable seating and no limit on how much food and drink I was allowed. As a non-drinker, perhaps I had a slight handicap. The lounge public address systems paged passengers when they should make their way to their gate; it was cool having my name called, which made me resolve to join the Qantas frequent flyer club on return.

My flight was QF21 departing at 9:55 p.m. As I sat at the gate lounge waiting for the announcement to board, I noticed a Japanese man watching me with a series of curious glances. Next to him was a women and it was obvious the two were a couple. I had denim jeans and a Detroit Tigers dugout jacket on and perhaps there was still remnants of a baseball player in my physique. We made eye contact, I smiled and said hello to him in Japanese, and he walked over to me. Whilst my Japanese was good enough for introductions, detailed chatting was beyond my skillset, but I did understand he was asking me if I played for the Tigers. I tried to tell him Australian pitcher Brad Thomas plays for the Tigers and he also played NPB and in the KBO. My Japanese obviously needed some work, because he became excited and called over his partner. Suddenly he had a camera in hand and a notepad with a pen for me to sign. I told him in English I was not Brad Thomas and repeated myself. However there was no stopping his wife from standing next to me beaming happily. Rather than attempt to explain I wasn't a star I decided to smile instead. They swapped places and we were photographed together and he thanked me in English several times and nodded as I signed my name on his notepad.

They were newlyweds probably in their late twenties, and I saw in his black folder some wedding photos around Sydney landmarks such as the Harbour Bridge.

Mistaken identity had given them a buzz, but their idea of Brad Thomas was about fifteen centimetres shorter than his actual height and I had a bit of puppy fat around my face, which meant the Brad Thomas they met had a double chin instead of one. I thought to myself that if I was half as talented as Brad Thomas on the pitching mound, I'd be very pleased with myself.

My boarding pass caused a light to flash on the machine scanner at the gate when the hostess processed it. I wondered why that had happened and I hoped I wouldn't be whisked away. The thought of a strip search and a large man or women with a rubber glove sent a nervous pulse through me. But then the hostess smiled and said, "You've been upgraded to a sky bed for this leg of your journey." I couldn't believe my luck, and the first thing I thought to say was, "Qantas is the best airline in the world! Thank you." The hostess laughed softly and replied, "We try to be."

The fact I was flying at a time which included my usual sleep hours meant there was a possibility I might be able to sleep for close to all of the nine hours and thirty-five minutes of flying time. Having a sky bed was such a bonus and I felt so excited to be starting my holiday in style.

Even though Japan was only a transit stop on the way home, I planned to spend two nights in Tokyo. I've been lucky to see so much of the world, and Japan was going to be a new experience for me.

I had about a five-hour wait at Tokyo Narita International Airport for the connecting flight to New York. For the first time I wouldn't be stopping on the West Coast, and it was exciting to think that I was crossing the Pacific Ocean and America in one flight. I sat in the gate lounge watching television news for most of my wait.

Japan Airlines Flight 6 departed Tokyo at 11:20 a.m. on June 24, and I would reach New York's JFK International at 11:25 a.m., also on June 24. The International Dateline is quite a trickster, as my actual flying time was thirteen hours and five minutes, yet according to date and time, only five minutes actually passed.

After about eight hours of flying we reached the West Coast of the US and I was thrilled to be back in American sky. Making my fifth trip to the US and fourth to the mainland, a part of me felt strongly connected to the place, as though I was returning to my second homeland.

I was wide awake the whole way across America, and I knew each time I looked out the window below me, there was probably something to do with baseball going on: a high school team training, a professional club gearing up for the day ahead and plenty of people watching morning news or reading a newspaper with baseball as part of the subject matter. I felt a real sense of belonging.

Getting through customs at JFK was surprisingly quick. Perhaps the timing of our flight meant we caught a break between other arrivals. I grabbed my luggage from the carousel and hailed a New York City yellow taxi. I had booked a room at the Holiday Inn Express Fifth Avenue on 13 West 45th Street, right near Times Square. I'd be staying there from Friday the twenty-fourth until Monday the twenty-seventh. Once in the taxi and on my way in a matter of minutes, I could see the skyline of New York City and wanted to jump up and down with excitement. We had a pretty good run, but things slowed down as we got into the city itself. I didn't mind. I was so happy to be back there. Silly as it may sound, when I got into my hotel room I jumped up and down on my king-size bed a few times. The last time I did that in a hotel room I was about ten years old and the ceiling was a lot further away from my head.

Part of the deal with my room was that I was entitled to one large pizza with two toppings and one two-litre bottle of soft drink per day. You've got to love the Americans—you'll never go hungry on their watch.

One of the first things I did once fully settled in was book tickets to the Yankees versus Colorado Rockies game on Saturday, June 25. I splashed out and purchased a ticket in section 119, row 14, and seat number 7. It didn't come cheap at $325 USD, yet it was a small price to pay to see a team play which I had followed since first becoming interested in baseball. I also organised a ticket each for Chris Vaccaro and his brother Bryan in section 217, row 19, and seats 1–2.

As I had made separate purchases for the tickets, I received a phone message in my room (I used my hotel contact details when booking the tickets online) from American Express USA wishing to confirm my transactions. It took me by surprise, but I was grateful they were alerted to what appeared to be abnormal spending. I rang the consultant back and explained it was all fine.

As I lay in bed that night full of pepperoni pizza and Pepsi, a sense of excitement raced through me with a warm buzz. I was going to Yankee Stadium!

Visiting the Bronx meant I would tick off my fourth of New York's five boroughs, with Staten Island the only one left to experience.

Excitement set in from the minute I woke up on June 25, and I smiled like a child on Christmas Day. Whilst there were other subway stations closer to my hotel I could have taken, I wandered a bit and found a horde of fans in Yankees gear walking through Times Square. I asked them if they were going to the game and they all said yes with plenty of enthusiasm. So I tagged along and boarded the same subway train as them. I didn't pay attention to the name of the subway station we went into, but finding my way back seemed quite simple as I had so many major landmarks right near my hotel.

It didn't seem to take too long to reach the field, perhaps about half an hour, and the stairs from the subway up to street level brought me face to face with the new Yankee Stadium. There was a gleam to the massive structure, with fresh paint and smooth surfaces proof of its infancy. A part of me rued not having experienced the old stadium, but the Yankees are the Yankees wherever they play. The former ground, though, had so much history, but an MLB franchise of perennial success like the Yankees, with twenty-seven World Series championships, was bound to etch the pages of baseball history with a lot more.

I found my seat easily, and there weren't many people there as it was more than two hours till game time. The seats are a similar shade to Yankees' navy blue, with a Yankees logo on the end of each row marker number. I certainly felt I had received my money's worth as there was only one section ahead of me, which was quite small because it was very exclusive and no doubt super pricey, yet I was close enough to call out to the players and be heard. My view was slightly from the first base side, directly behind home plate, with that thin section of seats probably only ten rows deep buffering me and the backstop fence. The Rockies were taking batting practice still, so it was nice to walk in and see Major Leaguers taking some swings with the hitting cage catching foul balls.

The jumbo television screen in centre field was active leading up to the game and caught my attention when it showed footage of an old-timers game from the previous day. I instantly recognised Aussie Graeme Lloyd and felt excitement he had just been there so recently, but disappointment I'd missed him by only one day.

My mind kicked into gear remembering Australian players associated with the Yankees. Right-handed pitcher Mark Hutton from Adelaide, South Australia, became the first Aussie to debut for the Yankees on July 23, 1993. He played at the Major League level from 1993–1994 and 1996, but was traded on July 31, 1996, to the Florida Marlins for David Weathers, which meant he wasn't on the Yankees World Series championship team for that year.

Any Australian reaching the Majors is a significant achievement, given the lower profile of the sport in Australia, but to have one appear on a team which is an international sporting brand is a very big deal. People all over the world who don't even follow baseball know a Yankees cap when they see one and to have an Aussie become part of this franchise was huge.

A Yankees cap is more than a piece of baseball-playing attire as it is an iconic symbol of American popular culture and people around the globe wear Yankees headwear knowing it is all-American. It is incredible that Hutton's hard work as a pitcher gave him the opportunity to be part of something with such far-reaching dimensions.

Hutton's steps in Yankees pinstripes made history for Australia in several ways. His debut on July 23, 1993, also marked the first occasion an Aussie started a Major League game as a pitcher, and he engraved the beginning of his Major League career in gold by pitching eight innings for just three hits and the win.

His move to the National League during the 1996 season yielded notable success. He had five wins and one loss, with an ERA of 3.67 over 56.1 innings pitched for the Marlins. He was traded to the Colorado Rockies on July 27, 1997, for Craig Counsell, and he also missed the chance to participate in the World Series that year, which the Marlins won. On December 10, 1997, he was traded by the Rockies to the Cincinnati Reds for Curtis Goodwin. Interestingly, Goodwin has an Australian link. He was an import outfielder for the Perth Heat during the 1993/1994 ABL season. He had a batting average of .319 and participated in 56 games, accumulating 188 at-bats. With sixty hits and thirty-two stolen bases, he always looked like a player on his way to the Majors. Hutton played his last game at the Major League level on May 21, 1998, with the Cincinnati Reds.

He enjoyed getting to bat in the National League, though, because in twenty-three at-bats he had seven hits, including one home run, which gave him a career batting average of .304. Hutton made history with each Major League club he played for because he was the first Aussie Yankee, Marlin, Rockie, and Red.

He played a season in the ABL for the Adelaide Giants during the 1994/1995 season. He had five wins and two losses, with an ERA of 5.33, over fifty-four innings pitched and struck out fifty-six batters. I met him once at Parramatta Stadium when he came to Sydney to play the Blues. At 1.98 metres tall and over 100 kilograms, I was up to about his knees back then. He autographed a ball for me and his signature was one of my favourites with its smooth flow and the clear legibility of his name. He had a big handlebar moustache that Australian summer, which made him look even scarier for a teenage pipsqueak like me, yet he seemed like a kind person who gave me earnest eye contact, followed by a shy smile and a pat on the back when I told him I wanted to be a New York Yankee like him one day.

It was fantastic to have him pitch for Australia at the Sydney 2000 Olympic Games. He was given the ball against heavyweight teams Japan for the round-robin game on September 19 and the USA for the round-robin game on September 24. He pitched a total of seven innings across both the games.

Graeme Lloyd missed Hutton by twenty-three days when he was traded to the Yankees on August 23, 1996. It was a slightly complicated trade. Lloyd and fellow Brewer Pat Listach, and a Brewers player to be named later, were traded for Gerald Williams and Bob Wickman from the Yankees. The player to be named later was Brewers all-star pitcher Ricky Bones.

Whilst there have been many great achievements by Australians who have played Major League Baseball, one that is perhaps the utmost individual performance belongs to Lloyd. It was game four of the 1996 World Series against the Atlanta Braves on October 23, 1996. It was the ninth inning, and the situation was certainly a tough one for the Yankees as the Braves had two runners on base, and they needed two outs to send the game into extra innings with the score locked at six all. But if the Braves scored a runner they would win the game and be one win away from claiming back-to-back World Series. It wasn't the first time Lloyd had been called upon during the Series to do a very difficult job, yet he was proving to be a secret weapon, and when he got Braves slugger Fred McGriff to ground into an inning-ending double play, he had done his job to perfection.

There are many defining moments in a player's career, and if fans of baseball didn't know who Lloyd was before the 1996 World Series he would be impossible to forget after game four. He pitched the first out at the bottom of the tenth, facing another heavy hitter, Ryan Klesko, for no damage, and then Series Most Valuable Player John Wetteland recorded the last two outs of the tenth. The Yankees won the game 8–6, and Lloyd made even more history for Australia. Not only was he the first Australian to play in a World Series, he was the winning pitcher in game four, something no other Aussie pitcher has achieved to date. He also had a World Series at-bat, which didn't result in a base hit, but it was another piece of history, and he was the first Australian to be on a World Series Championship team when the Yankees claimed the series by winning game six 3–2, on October 26, 1996.

I watched the series on television back in 1996, and remember game four and much of the series went late on school nights—but feeling tired for school was completely worth seeing Lloyd step up to so many challenges and succeed. The image of the Yankees' dugout when he got McGriff to hit into the double play was so jubilant, and all the high fives and pats on the back are among my all-time favourite baseball memories.

Lloyd was also part of another Yankees World Series Championship team when they clinched the 1998 series against the San Diego Padres. It could have been a treble, as the Yankees took the 1999 series, but he was part of a notable trade to the Toronto Blue Jays on February 18, 1999, instead. He was traded by the Yankees, with David Wells and Homer Bush, in exchange for Roger Clemens. It was clearly a reflection of Lloyd's value that he was part of a deal to bring one of the American League's most dominating pitchers of the 1980s and 1990s to the Yankees, being Clemens.

The trade included an ABL link too, as American Homer Bush was an import infielder for the Brisbane Bandits during the 1993/1994 season. He was the ABL's Most Valuable Player for that season, with a batting average of .374 in 50 games, with 67 hits in 179 at-bats, and 19 stolen bases. Bush's season in Australia also included being on the Brisbane Bandits ABL Championship Series winning team. Like Curtis Goodwin, it was clear he would go on to play in the Majors.

To date, Lloyd is the only Australian to have played for both the New York Yankees and the Mets, as he spent part of the 2003 season with the Mets. He is also the only Aussie to have played on both Canadian Major League clubs; in 1999, he pitched for the Blue Jays, and in 2001 and part of the 2002 season he pitched for the Montreal Expos.

During the Athens 2004 Olympic Games, Lloyd was the oldest Australian baseball participant at 37 years and 129 days old, yet having one of the country's most successful baseball players on the team was an incredible bonus. He participated in three round-robin games; first against Japan on August 18, followed by Greece on August 20, and Canada on August 22. Across those three games, he pitched two innings and was tasked with getting important outs often against left-handed hitters, which was consistent with the bedrock of his Major League career with lefty on lefty match-ups and also as a respected setup man. Lloyd pitched an inning in the gold medal game against Cuba on August 25. I didn't realise it at the time, but it would be the last time I would ever see him pitch in a game. Like the 1996 World Series, he was called upon to do a difficult job and struck out one batter and kept the mighty Cubans quiet with no damage. Lloyd is a sporting hero to me and no matter how big the challenge, he performed diligently and with such gentlemanly composure.

Even though Australia was defeated by the Cubans 6–2, the game was much closer than the end score reflected. With two baseball World Series rings and an Olympic silver medal, Lloyd is Australia's most decorated baseball player of all time.

Reminiscing about Australia's association with the Yankees, with all of Lloyd's and Hutton's achievements on the baseball field still fresh on my mind, made me feel like I was on a pilgrimage.

June 25, 2011, was a great day for a baseball game. There were some fluffy white clouds drifting across the horizon, with blue sky shining between. It was warm, and wearing a T-shirt was a smart decision as I had considered wearing a long-sleeved shirt.

I knew that Yankee Derek Jeter was out injured, but part of me hoped that June 25 might be the day he was back on the field. Alas, it wasn't, and I felt some disappointed that I was finally at a Yankees game and wasn't going to see Jeter play. He was so close to hit number three thousand, and perhaps if he hadn't had the misfortune of an injury, I might have seen him make a few hits toward that magical mark.

The Yankees are a team which never skimps on talent and when one player is unavailable there are several more stars to marvel at. Every player on a Major League roster is a highly skilled athlete, but in every direction I looked, the Yankees gave me a treat. Brett Gardner and Curtis Ganderson roamed the outfield. Mark Teixeira, Alex Rodriguez, and Robinson Cano had plenty of the infield covered; Jorge Posada was the designated hitter; and C. C. Sabathia was on the mound. I feel bad for not mentioning every player in the starting line-up, but I have followed quite closely the careers of the players mentioned above, and something inside me said that C. C. was going to pitch a good game.

The Colorado Rockies had some talent on their team too, and to be able to see franchise player Todd Helton, super shortstop Troy Tulowitzki, and Jason Giambi play certainly added plenty to the occasion. It came as no surprise Giambi received some boos when he was announced as their designated hitter, yet these boos contained some affection, as if to say, "We're jeering because you were our boy once, and we don't want you hitting a game winning home run today."

I knew when I saw Greg Maddux pitch back in 2004 I was witnessing a special talent do what he does best, but I rank seeing C. C. Sabathia highly too. C. C. pitched eight innings, for one earned run, he struck out nine batters, and took the win in a game the Yankees won 8–3. A total of 46,900 spectators attended the game, and together we can say we saw C. C. throw a gem.

I got my money's worth in every way, as there was plenty of hitting too. For the Yankees, Granderson, Teixeira, Rodriguez, Swisher, Posada, and Cervelli all had a multihit game. Teixeira hit a home run in the eighth inning, and I wondered how many the slugger would hit for his whole career. I hope he smacks five hundred or more because it would be pleasing to know that I saw with my own eyes part of such an impressive tally. No matter how many he puts over the fence, he's a super player and just to be at a game with him on the field is something to fondly remember. The Yankees had fifteen hits in that game.

Tulowitzki worked hard as per usual with two hits, and Wigginton slogged a home run for the Rockies in the ninth inning. As a team they had eight hits, but the Yankees scored two runs in the first inning and three in the third, which made it quite a bumpy start for the Rockies. All of the Rockies' runs came in the last two innings of the game. It was just one of those days where everything boomed for the Yankees.

I met Chris and Bryan Vaccaro at their seats when the game finished. It had been close to eight months since I had last seen Chris and I was meeting Bryan for the first time. Chris introduced me to Bryan and given his massive interest in baseball, it was fitting our first encounter be at a Major League ballpark.

We decided to catch up over a meal at the Hard Rock Café, which adjoins the stadium at Gate Six on the corner of 161st Street and River Avenue. At first it looked completely full, but Bryan had his sporting speed and instincts in tune, and in a flash he was seated at a high table with three chairs, with his arms in the air to direct Chris and I. The previous patrons of the table were still within arm's reach of Bryan, yet he looked like he had been sitting there all day long. "That was impressive," I said to him gratefully. Chris had told me in e-mail correspondence Bryan played baseball and was a leader on his high school team, and was hoping for a college opportunity later in 2011. He looked as fit as a racehorse, trim and toned with good reach to him and appeared to be about 1.83 metres tall. "I'm going to call you the Jock from now on, you're a natural athlete." He gave a modest laugh in reply.

We spent some time recapping the game and Teixeira's home run was a point of some discussion as we all agreed on the reliability of his bat and glove.

The next point of discussion was going over the details for me to get to Holtsville, Long Island, as this was their home suburb and I was staying at the Crowne Plaza there from June 27–July 3. Chris wrote out all the details in terms of what transportation I needed to take to get there, it was great we were going to be hanging out for close to a week. On June 30, we planned to drive down to Reading, Pennsylvania, where I had organised a press pass for us both with the AA minor league team the Reading Phillies and the chance to interview Perth, West Australian Tim Kennelly, who played for Reading, and Australian-born Clayton Tanner, a pitcher for the visiting Richmond Flying Squirrels. Part of me hoped that over the next week neither of these two players would be suddenly called up to AAA or the Majors, as I had travelled a long way.

CHAPTER 7
CLAYTON TANNER

Grand Central Terminal on 89 East 42nd Street at Park Avenue was a comfortable walk from my hotel, even with luggage. I took the Metropolitan Transportation Authority, Long Island Rail Road to Ronkonkoma, and enjoyed seeing the suburbs flashing by during the journey. I had a few seconds to take in my surroundings before another suburb filled my window. It was a short taxi ride to the Crowne Plaza Holtsville. The driver told me he had friends from Queensland, Australia, who were part of an Internet discussion group he's a member of, and one day he hoped to visit them.

Chris's timetable was quite favourable during my time there and we were able to visit several of his favourite spots. Sachem High School is a sacred place for him. He was a sports editor/writer at the school for four years and he graduated from Sachem in 2004. Chris earned a varsity letter for track and field. In 2008, his book, *Sachem High School Football: The History of the Flaming Arrows*, was published. These days, amongst his many duties as a journalist, he is the media editor/writer for the *Sachem Arrows*.

The Arrows' home field is named Fred Fusaro Alumni Stadium in honour of the legendary head coach, whose tenure was from 1971–2002, and in 2003 Fusaro served as the special assistant to help the new coach. Chris took me on a walking tour of it and the artificial grass was like nothing I'd seen in Australia. I've seen plenty of Astroturf in my time, but this stuff included synthetic grass blades. With the freezing weather in the northeast of America during their winter, it made sense to use a surface which could cope better with the elements.

The next day, Chris, his girlfriend Theresa, and I enjoyed the beautiful summer weather and went to Smith Point Beach, a short drive away. The glaring sun was a welcome change from the grey winter back in Sydney. Smith Point Beach reminded me of Australia, except we would never have a car park of stadium capacity there, but I wish we did. Town planning for parking around Australian metropolitan beaches doesn't involve much thought at all, and the metered parking bays are expensive. But the white sand, the thirty-to fifty-metre width of Smith Point Beach at various sections, and the one-to two-metre swell gently rolling in all combined to form a picture similar to beaches between Newcastle and Port Macquarie on Australia's New South Wales Mid-Northern Coast.

We also caught up at the beach with Chris's brother and his girlfriend Amanda. The two of them look like sports Barbie and Ken with their tall, toned, tanned, athletic frames and cheerful smiles. Saying good-bye to them for the afternoon, I said, "It was nice to see you both Mr. and Mrs. Jock." They laughed in reply.

On June 29, Theresa's younger sister Melissa, who I attended the Mets game with in 2010 and their teenage brother Frankie-Joe joined Chris and I for a drive to some of the most eastern points of Long Island. Theresa couldn't come because of work commitments. Melissa and Frankie-Joe played this game where they punched each other on the arm when they saw a car with a licence plate from outside New York. "Connecticut!" Punch... "Rhode Island!" Punch!

The Twin Forks of Long Island is a distinctive feature of the land's eastern geography, and we were about as eastward as we could go at the Montauk Point Lighthouse. It was constructed in 1796, and part of me became lost in a trance knowing that the lighthouse was over two hundred years old, making it the first one in New York state. It was commissioned by President George Washington, which added to the sense of history. I wondered how many ships it had provided safe passage to. I appreciated from the top vantage point that I was sharing the same view of the North Atlantic Ocean as people from a few centuries ago. The coastal area near the lighthouse didn't seem to have been developed. Some of the vegetation had probably been cleared in the past and perhaps the green foliage and small beaches which skirted the front of the lighthouse were perhaps a legacy of a time long ago.

We were back in Holtsville by early evening as Chris and I planned to drive across a few state lines to reach Reading, Pennsylvania, on June 30. I went to bed early, knowing the following day would present me with some unique and special opportunities.

The chance to visit the Reading Phillies had come about because Anthony Burkhart, a sports reporter at the *Pottsville Republican & Herald*, wrote an article featuring Aussie Tim Kennelly on May 2, 2011. I reached out to Burkhart by e-mail, and told him I enjoyed his story and we established a dialogue from there. As a utility, Kennelly has played infield and outfield positions and his ability to come up with a clutch hit or a big play had caught Burkhart's attention. It was inconceivable during the 2010/2011 ABL season for me to foresee I would be visiting him in Reading, yet a bit of initiative had made it possible.

Burkhart referred me to the R-Phillies director of PR and media relations, Tommy Viola and Chris and I had a media field credential for FirstEnergy Stadium waiting for us. We crossed state lines for New York, New Jersey, and Pennsylvania on our way, which added two new states to my places visited in the US.

From the moment I met Viola, his enthusiasm and professionalism shined. He was up in the stadium's broadcasting box when we were walked up and introduced to him by a ground attendant. I could tell he had about ten different tasks to see to as he had meticulously laidout paperwork in front of him and broadcasting equipment was being set up, yet he stopped what he was doing, giving us his full attention, followed by a welcoming smile and a handshake.

Like any important meeting with an American baseball dignitary, I made sure I had a pack of Tim Tams and a block of Cadbury chocolate as welcoming gifts. The heat that day was quite heavy, even though the sun was only bright as opposed to blazing. "You should throw those in the fridge before they melt, the Tim Tams are amazing when frozen," I suggested.

"Will do, and thank you for thinking of me." Viola showed us some of the stadium's features as we walked down to the home dugout while the visiting Richmond Flying Squirrels were completing some throwing and drill work. The R-Phillies and FirstEnergy Stadium are a beating heart of baseball, which gives a town like Reading a team to follow that is often loaded with up-and-coming Phillies prospects. There was a hint of a recent makeover to the stadium, with glistening fresh paint on many of the walls, the grass on the field was cut to perfection, bright sponsorship signage skirted the outfield wall, outdoor bars and dining areas looked straight out onto the field, brass bands were preparing for the evening, and behind the centre field fence the smooth green hill lined with trees on the top was a pretty backdrop. Not far from the stadium, there were more green rolling hills, giving the place a natural freshness.

Chris setup his video camera and we briefly waited as Viola asked one of the coaching staff to bring Tim Kennelly out. I felt a rush of excitement just standing there on the picturesque field with so many good players walking past, and some had Big League experience.

Kennelly walked up through the dugout entrance and paused with surprise when he saw me standing there with Chris and Viola on the field. "What are you doing here?"

"I'm here to interview you." I had a shoulder bag with me, and during that short pause I retrieved a packet of Tim Tams and a block of Cadbury chocolate for him. I laughed and said, "Here's a little something from home for you." His face turned into a big smile, and he said, "Oh, you legend!" and he shook my hand. Knowing it was quite warm outside, he asked one of the bat boys to put the home loot in his locker for later consumption.

It was my first video interview and the only other person who knew that was Chris. I tried to act confidently, as a local news crew looked on, and I hoped to do okay. Chris was good for my nerves as he had a lot of experience with video interviews and his energy was constantly positive. "Don't worry, you'll do fine," he kept saying. I did make a couple of rookie errors. I wanted the backdrop of the beautiful field, but the wind had picked up, there was chatter from players around us, and stadium music was blaring, so there was some noise interference. I probably had too much of an active voice as Kennelly spoke. I wanted to try to cover both ABL and R-Phillies experiences and it came together quite nicely.

American pitcher Cole McCurry was on the Perth Heat team during the 2010/2011 ABL season, as an import from the Baltimore Orioles organisation he was quoted as saying he went into spring training after the ABL season feeling like his arm was at midseason strength. His comment was a positive endorsement for the ABL, and so I began there with Kennelly and asked him how he felt going into spring training. "The at-bats, ground balls, and fly balls are all helpful coming back over here for spring training," he said.

Kennelly had participated in the Phillies 2011 Major League spring training with so many excellent players around him including Jimmy Rollins. News came back to Australia he had stood his own, and I was keen to hear what he had to say about it.

"I think I got an RBI double in my first at-bat, and that was huge…" he said, implying that it was a big moment for him. I always find it pleasing to see a player step up to an occasion, and the fact that Kennelly was hitting safely in the Major League camp meant he had the skills to perhaps do the job at that level.

He had proven himself a utility to the fullest extent when he pitched for the R-Phillies a few weeks before my interview, and it was pleasing to extract some of the details from him:

"We were actually in Portland, Maine…I think it might have been in May, we were losing by ten runs in the ninth inning, I was in the bullpen warming up some of the guys… a phone call came down to the pen 'get Kennelly going'…I still had my shin guards on…I threw about five pitches… then I looked out and saw the manager walking toward the mound…I threw one pitch, one out, and got the guy to fly out…It was exciting, but it went pretty quick."

The way Kennelly smiled when he talked, and his comfortable body language, helped me to realise just how much he enjoyed playing and regardless of whatever opportunity he was presented with, he liked to do the job for the team.

I liked the look of Reading and wanted to know what he thought of the place. "Playing in front of these fans is awesome," he said. "They're real good fans, we get a lot of fans each day…definitely compares up there with one of the best places I've played…"

We shook hands at the end of the interview, which I'd completed without too many hitches. It was great to have also done my first joint project with Chris as he was the videographer and editor. The final product is on YouTube, under "Tim Kennelly Interview, Reading Phillies, June 30, 2011, by VaccaroHenning." It is 8:32 minutes in duration.

The next leg of our visit was interviewing Clayton Tanner, which would prove to be a historic moment for baseball in Australia.

Tanner first came to my attention on the Australian Baseball News website ABL Buzz in 2010, which made me wonder why I hadn't heard of him until then, as he was born in Mona Vale, Sydney, New South Wales, on December 5, 1987, and had been playing minor league baseball within the San Francisco Giants organisation since 2006. Normally the signing of any Australian player is news well circulated within the Aussie baseball community. To know so little about Tanner made him quite a mystery.

A big clue as to why I hadn't heard of Tanner struck me when I learnt he was drafted by the San Francisco Giants in the third round of the 2006 MLB June amateur draft from

De La Salle High School, in Concord, California. I started to hypothesise that he would have spent his senior high school years there, which could explain why he'd slipped under the radar. This still didn't explain why a player of such talent had received so little baseball press in Australia.

I later discovered a couple of stories written by American sports writers regarding Tanner, dated from late 2010 into the early stages of the 2011 season. I learnt he was born in Australia, but had lived in the US almost his entire life. It was a sense of adventure which brought his mother Kim to Australia and a vacation became a long stay. They made it back to Sydney, for a holiday when Clayton was thirteen years old, for the 2000 Olympic Games.

Viola spoke to a media staffer travelling with the Richmond Flying Squirrels, but after about twenty minutes of waiting, Chris and I decided to walk over to the visitors' clubhouse entrance. A Flying Squirrels player was about to walk in so I asked for his help, saying, "Excuse me, mate, could you do a favour for me?"

"Sure," he replied, and I wish I had taken note of his jersey number or learnt his name because he was a good help.

"I've come from Australia to interview Clayton Tanner. Could you please let him know we're hoping to catch up with him for a few minutes?"

"No problem," he said smiling.

"Thank you for your assistance."

A few minutes later there was Tanner standing in front of us. All I knew of him came from written text as I hadn't found any video interviews on the Internet so I didn't even know the sound of his voice. He stood slightly taller than I was expecting, at about 1.88 metres in height, looking as fit as a middle-distance runner with a slim, toned physique. He appeared surprised we had called for him, yet he had a welcoming warm grin.

"Hello, Clayton, it's great to meet you, do you have time for a short interview to go back to Australia?"

"Sure." We shook hands and he walked with us back toward the field where the video camera was set up. While Chris attended to the camera for a few moments, I took the opportunity to tell Tanner a bit about myself and my books. I gave him my business card and said "I've got some things from Australia for you," retrieving Tim Tams and Cadbury chocolate. I also had a photo book of Manly, Sydney, for him too. "Thank you," he said, sounding pleased with his Aussie stash. I flicked through the picture book, and there were a couple of aerial shots where you could just see the roofs of Mona Vale Hospital. I pointed to it and said, "That's where you were born, mate." He took a moment to look at it carefully.

I was about to start the interview when a rock band which was part of the venue entertainment started a rehearsal right behind us. "Sorry, we'll have to take this back over toward the visiting team club house," I said with a hint of frustration. It only took us a few minutes to get set up in the dining area close to the left field outfield foul line, which provided a great view of Tanner with the field behind him. The only problem was that there was still a bit of background noise as staff arranged cooking and serving utensils, which caused plenty of banging and clunking sounds. I decided we just had to put up with it, realising it wasn't easy locating the quietest spot on a baseball field.

As we prepared to get rolling, I confirmed with Tanner he hadn't been interviewed by anyone from Australia and proudly told him an Aussie exclusive was about to get underway.

I began by asking him if his birth in Mona Vale, Sydney, Australia, was a talking point, as a kid, among his friends in California.

He said, “Nobody would really know it until someone mentions Australia…and you happen to mention you’re from there…they don’t necessarily believe you at first being in California…It definitely came up and it was cool, and they found it interesting…” It was nice to know that his birth in such a faraway place from where he grew up generated plenty of talk.

I wondered if reminiscing on old times in Australia had come up during family conversations, and this became my next question for him.

“The biggest thing is my mom, she lived there for like seven years, she travelled the whole world, Australia was her favourite place…my memories are pretty vague, it’s nice to hear all the stories.”

Ever since Tanner became known to Australian fans, the burning question so many people, including myself, wanted to know was if he was interested in playing in the Australian Baseball League.

“I just found out about it this spring training and, ah, it’s something exciting that I’ll hopefully get to experience…”

Finally, perhaps the biggest question was finding out how he felt about potentially representing Australia in the green and gold. It was another country, but the country he was born in, and at that moment it really hit me what an exclusive interview I had.

“Growing up in the States, mostly you like to play for the United States but at the same time, as you said, I’m originally from Australia, and that would be a great honour to wear the colours and be able to represent them at the world level.”

The full interview with Tanner is on YouTube and is 5:09 minutes in duration. Like Kennelly, I found him to be a very pleasant person, it was pleasing to be able to deliver to baseball fans in Australia the first-ever Aussie interview involving him. For administrators of the ABL and Team Australia, the interview provided them with confirmation of his interest. Most importantly, he at last had a voice and a presence people in Australia could see on the screen. It took some effort for Chris and I to get there to interview him, yet it was so worth it.

We would have liked to have stayed and watched the game that night, but wanted to get ahead of the peak-hour traffic back to New York. We left having made our bit of history and keen to e-mail it to Australian Baseball news services, which we did within a day.

Tommy Viola, who was a fantastic help for us, became the PR/media relations director for the Charlotte Knights, the AAA affiliate for the Chicago White Sox, in 2012. Having an Aussie on his club followed him because fastball relief pitcher Shane Lindsay from Melbourne re-joined the White Sox organisation from the Chicago Cubs on June 29, 2012, and he was assigned to Charlotte. I'm hoping Viola's next move is to the Major Leagues.

I departed New York on July 3 for two nights in Las Vegas, cursed with a morning flight at 7:20 a.m. from La Guardia, American Airlines 305, which flew via Chicago O'Hare with a few hours stopover. The early start meant I reached Las Vegas McCarran International Airport at 11:50 a.m., and used most of the day to explore. I walked much of the Las Vegas Strip and marvelled at the colour and decadence of so many hotels and casinos. It was amusing to see a replica of the Eiffel Tower and the Statute of Liberty on the same road.

The MGM Grand Hotel and Casino had plenty of character, with a massive gold lion statue on display out the front and the three letter logo was in big white letters high above the building's main structure. The Bellagio water fountain dancing feature was fun to watch, I remembered the final group scene in the remake film *Ocean's Eleven* where they're all standing there, knowing their heist was a success.

I experienced my first Independence Day in Las Vegas. It was everything I could have hoped for and I spent the day shopping at the Las Vegas Premium Outlets North at Iron Horse Drive and Grand Central Parkway. I ended up with bags full of clothes and perfume at great discounts. Baseball was front of my mind, when I picked up a Boston Red Sox cap and two Red Sox T-shirts for my good friend John McRae, and New York Yankees attire for another good mate, Andrew Hoysted. The night sky was filled with fireworks and the light and flashes bounced off the glass windows of the many hotels and casinos, making the Strip look like an even brighter glitter of ever changing colour.

I am a magnet to morning flights because American Airlines 1075 departed for Los Angeles at 6:50 a.m. on July 5, and even at that time of the day, it was warm in Las Vegas. I landed in Los Angeles at 7:55 a.m. and transferred onto American Airlines 169, which took off for Tokyo, Japan, at 11:50 a.m. I had a few hours to wait, so I had a nap in the departure gate lounge.

It was eleven hours and twenty-five minutes flying time to Tokyo, Narita International Airport, and I slept for nearly the entire flight. I landed there at 3:15 p.m. on July 6, 2011. Perhaps my most memorable experience in Japan was getting awakened that night because it felt like a giant hand was shaking my bed and I suddenly realised it was either an earthquake or an aftershock. I waited for an alarm to be sounded at the hotel, but there was nothing except night silence, and all the lighting and everything else seemed normal. Part of me wondered if I had dreamt it, yet it was an unmistakeable vibration which travelled through my whole body. Some people might consider such an event frightening, but I felt somewhat excited to have experienced such incredible force from nature.

I was so pleased my flight back to Australia was during the evening at 8:30 p.m. on board Qantas Flight 22, nonstop to Sydney. Even though I had enjoyed a fantastic holiday, it was great to be heading home.

Back in Sydney, I received two surprises within a few weeks of each other. The first was my dad phoning me to say he had collected a parcel from America for me from our post office box. I was thrilled and surprised to open it to find a 1995 Edition Starting Lineup Sports Superstar Collectibles still-boxed figurine and baseball card of Dave Nilsson. While many baseball cards feature Australian players, this was the first toy that I knew of an Aussie, which made it more like an artifact. I had mentioned to Chris Vaccaro during the drive back from Reading how I was frustrated I couldn't find an American seller on Amazon.com who would ship me the figurine. Chris's thoughtfulness made my day and I doubt if many collectors in Australia own such a unique item, but I do thanks to my mate.

The next unexpected event was receiving an e-mail from Clayton Tanner and conversing with him over several e-mails. His enthusiasm to play for Team Australia was as strong as he stated during the Reading interview and I referred him to the ABL's General Manager Ben Foster. A short time later he received an e-mail from Team Australia's Field

Manager Jon Deeble and the possibility of Tanner playing in green and gold at the 2011 Baseball World Cup gained momentum.

I took the opportunity to learn more about Tanner, wanting fans in Australia to discover new things about him and I regularly fed details to Australian Baseball news services. On August 2, 2011 he responded to a series of questions from me, as the Baseball World Cup was approaching and I wanted to establish if he was going to play for Team Australia.

"I would love to be able to represent Australia in the World Cup this year, but I actually got some bad news last week. I was informed that no members of the forty-man roster are able to participate in the World Cup. As I am on the forty-man, I will not be able to attend. I will just have to wait for the World Baseball Classic and hope the team will need me and I will be called on to help them out. It is something that I very much look forward to."

It was certainly disappointing news. Baseball is a fast-moving game on and off the field and I received an e-mail from Tanner dated September 4, 2011 with some surprising news:

> The Giants designated me for assignment, which means they took me off the forty-man to make room for some other players. I was then released, so I was able to talk with other teams and decide who I wanted to play for. The Reds showed great interest and are a great organization, so I was thrilled to get a chance with them.
>
> I could not be happier with this new situation that I am in! I am thankful for everything the Giants did for me because without them, my life would be a lot different.

> However, I felt like it was time to make a change, and the Cincinnati organization is a great one to be with.
>
> My situation is a little more uncommon, as I signed with the team with only four games remaining. Usually you may sign in the off-season or closer to spring training so you can take your goals into camp with you. In my situation, my main goal right now is to finish the season strong here, and then go and have the best off-season of my career, getting my body into the best possible shape.
>
> Now that I am no longer on the forty-man, I am eligible to play for Australia in the World Cup, which is very exciting! As long as I can get all my passport details taken care of in time, we will be good to go!

When he referred to his passport, he was commenting on obtaining his Australian passport. The Reds put Tanner straight on their AAA team, Louisville and he appeared in one game. He pitched three innings in relief, for no runs, and he struck out four batters. It was certainly a positive beginning for him, just one level below the Majors and plenty of the batters he faced had Big League experience.

All the necessary documentation was completed, and Tanner joined Team Australia for the 2011 Baseball World Cup in Panama, which was played from October 1–15. I felt warm satisfaction knowing I'd played a very small hand in the process by putting him in contact with the right people. There was a hint of irony, though, because I had interviewed him and Tim Kennelly in Reading as opposing players, and now they were on the same team.

Tanner continued to spoil me with exclusive information. The World Cup was well underway on October 7, 2011 and he replied to four questions from me, which as per usual he agreed to let me furnish to Aussie Baseball News services.

I began by asking how he felt to be representing his country of birth.

"It is a great honor to be able to represent team Australia. Not only am I getting the opportunity to play for the place where I was born, but I am able to represent the entire country. It is a great honor, and I am truly thankful for the chance."

I wondered how this team full of Aussies compared to others that he had played on during his professional career.

"This team is like no other that I have ever played on. Obviously being that I have played for three different teams now just within the last two months, I have had a lot of change and met tons of different kinds of players and people. The vibe here in the clubhouse is great. Everyone on the team is very welcoming and very positive. It makes for a great atmosphere to play in and to try and win. Everyone here has been nothing but supportive of me, which has helped ease the transition to this team."

Getting an idea of how he rated the quality of Team Australia in terms of assigning a professional standard to it was my next question:

> It wouldn't be fair for me to try and assign a certain level of competition or quality to this team. We have such a range of experience on this team, all the way from Big League time down to just short season experience. That is one thing that I believe makes this team so unique, that everyone can learn so much from the person playing next to them. There is so much knowledge, whether

> it's from a teammate or one of the great coaches that we get the opportunity to play for. We have nothing but competitors in the clubhouse, with everyone having the same goal, and that is to not only win for the person next to us in the clubhouse, but to bring a championship back to Australia.

I felt moved by this response and gained some inspiration from his excellent perspective and choice of words.

With dual World Series Champion Graeme Lloyd on the coaching staff, my final question for Tanner was what it was like having him as a pitching coach:

> Having Lloydy as a pitching coach has been a real treat. Not only was he obviously able to get it done when he played, but he has a great way of connecting with the staff and passing on his wisdom of the game. He is very easy to talk to, and someone that you get along with both on and off the field. There are a lot of coaches that you come across that were great players, but don't necessarily have the skill to teach it or communicate it the right way with their players. With the combination of Lloydy and Phil Dale, it has been a great learning experience and an awesome staff to come into.

It was music to my ears hearing all those great comments about a person I admire and respect so deeply, and it was further proof of the remarkable man that is Graeme Lloyd.

Tanner made his Australian debut as the team's starting pitcher against South Korea on October 4, 2011. He then started for Australia against Germany on October 9, but the game he perhaps dreamed of pitching, and then actually did, was in round two against Team USA on October 13. Rain caused the game to be reduced in duration, but Tanner showed skill and deep determination by pitching six complete innings for only six hits, no earned runs, no walks and struck out four batters, whilst only facing twenty-two batters in his six innings of work. The final score was Team USA 2, Australia 1, and Tanner took the loss on two unearned runs, but what a fantastic way to rise to the occasion and give Australia a chance to beat the Americans at baseball! In my mind, he deserved the win for his tenacity, and his value as an ace on the Australian pitching staff had all the proof it needed.

Australia finished the World Cup by equalling its best ever placing of fifth.

Tanner's good nature and pitching talent made me want to learn even more about him, so I asked him to forward some questions to his mother Kim, as a mum knows all there is to know about her children and also to ascertain more about Kim's time in Australia. When I received a forwarded e-mail back from Kim dated April 21, 2012, the wonderful story of Kim and her son was going to a level that probably only family and friends were aware of.

I asked Kim what brought her to Sydney, Australia. She wrote: "In 1979, at nineteen years old, I decided I wanted to travel. My first adventure was a camping trip through Europe. There I met many other travellers, mostly Australians. I knew immediately my next destination was going to be to 'The Lucky Country'—Australia!! While I was in Europe, I met my very dear friend, Denise Featherston Booth. She was from Dee Why, on the Northern Beaches of Sydney, which soon became my home away from home. Six months turned into ten years!"

When I read this, I admired Kim for taking such an odyssey as a teenager and how a deep friendship began with a common interest of travel. I've done my fair share of travel, but I was in my twenties when I undertook solo journeys and never with a backpack on my back, taking shelter at campsites.

I'm always interested to know from people who visit Australia and stay for a while if there was an aspect of Australian culture that particularly captured their attention.

"There are many aspects of Australian culture that I enjoyed," she wrote. "From the original traditions of Aboriginal culture to the now multicultural diverseness that is Australia. From Australian art to Australian music; from Aussie barbecues and summer cricket games on the beach to surfing and sailing on the beautiful waters! Compared to the USA, life was a lot more relaxed and not as fast-paced. I loved that about Australia."

I asked Kim if she had a favourite Australian place or landscape.

"There are so many beautiful areas of Australia, but my favourites would have to be Sydney's Northern Beaches from Palm Beach to Manly," she said. "Also, I worked on the ship *Fairstar* for Stimar Cruises while I was there. We docked on many different harbors along the way, but hands down, Sydney Harbor was the most beautiful. And of course, I must say there is nothing like the Great Barrier Reef and the surrounding islands."

Knowing she returned with Clayton for the Sydney 2000 Olympic Games, I asked if she noticed any changes to Sydney since she was last there.

"The one change I noticed was more multiculturalism—others had discovered 'The Lucky Country!' But for the most part, I was amazed and pleased at how things had remained the same! My favourite little delis, restaurants, and shops were still there! Here in America, places continually come and go."

I moved the questions on to baseball and asked Kim how she felt when it was confirmed that Clayton would play for Australia at the Baseball World Cup.

"How did I feel…Complete pride and excitement! I couldn't believe that the little boy I had twenty-three years ago at Mona Vale Hospital was going to be representing Australia in the Baseball World Cup! What an accomplishment! Seeing photos of him wearing the Australian uniform… Wow! Absolutely amazing!!"

I continued along these lines and asked when Clayton was a boy, and even as a teenager, did she ever imagine that baseball would help further connect him to his country of birth.

"It was always my hope that Clayton would have a passion for Australia, his birth country," she said. "Clayton started playing baseball in Little League at age five and continued through high school, when his dream of becoming a professional baseball player was realized and he was drafted by the San Francisco Giants! I must say, not in my wildest dreams did I ever imagine his baseball career would lead him to represent and play for Team Australia."

My final question to Kim was to note that every person I had spoken to on Team Australia, and based on my own interaction with Clayton, said he is a true gentleman, and I asked what she attributed his excellent demeanour to.

"He takes after his mom, of course! Actually, Clayton reminds me that I was fairly strict with him. By strict, I mean consequences for actions. Good and bad. As a child and young man, Clayton has always been honest and hardworking. He has always been respectful toward others and takes nothing for granted. He is grateful for what he has been given. Those morals and values have not changed. I agree he is a true gentleman and a wonderful son!"

It was brilliant to be able to converse with Kim and what a lovely person.

Being from Sydney and knowing quite a few people within the professional baseball community, I was able to reach out to Tanner's World Cup roommate, fellow pitcher Todd Van Steensel. He played minor league baseball within the Philadelphia Phillies organisation in 2009 and likewise with the Minnesota Twins organisation in 2011. Van Steensel has a well-earned reputation as a good guy and I've always found him to be very hospitable. As someone who spent time with Tanner on and off the field, I was interested in learning about how they got on, and he kindly e-mailed me his responses to my questions on April 24, 2012.

"My first impression was that he was a pretty easy-going and relaxed guy, and on the field I noticed he was really focused and there was purpose to everything he did," Van Steensel said.

"He was a great roommate," he said. "I've had a lot of roommates in my time, and he's up there with the best of them. Since we spent a lot of time in the room we spoke a lot, and since he had spent time in MLB spring training and in AAA, I was always asking him questions of what it was like at those levels. He was always willing to answer and give me insight into the higher levels of professional baseball. We had similar interests so we always had something to laugh or joke about."

I wanted to learn more about his skills on the mound and asked Van Steensel accordingly.

"I first noticed he didn't have overpowering stuff, but he made his fastball cut and sink and he was able to spot up really well," Van Steensel said. "I would say he's a harder throwing version of Josh Spence." Spence is an Australian left-handed pitcher, like Tanner, who made his Major League debut on June 24, 2011, with the San Diego Padres.

I concluded by asking Van Steensel his lasting impression of Tanner from the World Cup. "He's a fun guy to be around and a good guy to have a conversation with, just an all-round top bloke."

What started as the first-ever interview with Tanner on behalf of Australia in Reading, Pennsylvania, became a special opportunity to learn a lot about him.

I know he would very much liked to have played in the ABL during the 2011/2012 season, but his preparation going into the 2012 season for his new organisation, the Reds, was first priority.

The 2011/2012 ABL season was special for many reasons, which included the ABL's debut in the 2011 Asia Series, where Australian champions the Perth Heat played against the championship teams of professional leagues from East Asia.

CHAPTER 8
THE 2011 ASIA SERIES

The 2011 Asia Series was held in Taiwan and took place from November 25–29, 2011, meaning it was scheduled during the first month of the 2011/2012 ABL season, which began on November 4, 2011.

Baseball's world profile continues to grow, and it is sometimes not realised by some fans how big the sport is in Asia. Countries like Japan, Taiwan and South Korea have immense passion for the game, and it's a national team sport in all of these countries. Consequently, Major League Baseball is seeing more of its international reach, with a steady flow of players coming from Asia.

It's also of note baseball in Asia isn't in competition with many other professional team sports, which means baseball often has top billing, with soccer as another team sport that is well supported, especially leading up to the Football World Cups. Both Japan and South Korea are also very capable on the soccer pitch.

The Asia Series is still somewhat in its infancy, with the inaugural tournament taking place in 2005 then a break in 2009 and 2010, before the series returned in 2011. The success of international club championships has been demonstrated by soccer with competitions like the Champions

League. Therefore, the Asia Series is very fertile ground for baseball to build up international club championships.

When I learnt the Perth Heat was going to participate in the 2011 series, it was a cause of excitement as the Heat would have an opportunity to test themselves against the championship team from the Nippon Professional Baseball league, the Korean Baseball Organization, and the Chinese Professional Baseball League. To put this in perspective, NPB is second only to MLB in terms of the standard of play, team payrolls, and the size of the league. The KBO and CPBL are also fully professional leagues with plenty of local players who have played MLB.

While the Perth Heat's 2011/2012 roster had players with AAA and MLB experience, there was also those who played for fun and had day jobs. Australian media was quick to reveal some on the Heat's team worked in factories and as retail shop assistants to earn an income, finding time for baseball around their occupation, in stark contrast to Luke Hughes, who was at the apex of the sport as a Major Leaguer. There was something very Australian about a team of hybrid baseball professionals taking on teams who had single players earning more playing baseball than the combined yearly income of all the Heat players who played professionally in the US. The sporting history of Australians taking on big challenges was presented by the Asia Series, but the Heat could take some confidence as the ABL champions and having not yet lost a game during the 2011/2012 ABL season.

If the Heat won the title, the team would pocket about $624,000 USD. If they finished second, they were looking at about $340,000 USD, and if they finished in either of the bottom two positions they could earn $100,000 USD for their effort. There were some slight variations in what the reported prize money was, my source was Paul Huang's article "CPBL: Asia Series to get under way after two-year hiatus," dated May 19, 2011, from the *Taipei Times*. Given that the tournament was to be held in Taiwan, he would certainly have been well informed.

The grandest of sporting fixtures all take time to build up in terms of profile and prestige, and spectator support. The Asia Series certainly has the potential to be a premier event on the international baseball calendar and this will only be achieved as it creates more of its own history. In time, team rivalries will develop; fans will fondly remember being witness to seeing their team in action; and the new memories will be created from great play with every series. Underpinning all of this is a sense of national pride, as not only are the championship teams representing their respective league clubs, but they are also playing for their countries.

The format of the 2011 Asia Series impressed me, as it all took place within a week, with each of the four teams playing each other once, and the teams placed first and second at the end of the round-robin stage faced off in the final. The tight schedule also meant players weren't committed for several weeks of work, which could reduce the likelihood of injuries.

The Perth Heat had a reverse season situation compared to the other teams, as the Heat had just started their 2011/2012 season and the rest had just finished theirs. This could be an advantage or a disadvantage, as on the one hand the Heat were fresh coming into a season, allowing them some time to work on finding the right team form and rhythm, but it could be argued that having a full season of baseball behind a team was a stronger position to be in. Either way, the Heat had to go out there and do their best to try and match the champions of Asia, which was an exciting challenge.

The Fukuoka SoftBank Hawks were the champions from NPB; the Samsung Lions were the KBO's best; and the Uni-President 7-Eleven Lions were the winners from the CPBL. On a good day, I felt the Heat was capable of beating all of them, yet as long as they were competitive I wasn't so concerned with whether they won, lost, or drew. It was a bit of an ominous tournament history that an NPB team had won each of the previous titles from 2005–2008.

I followed the series through the electronic media and cable television, but one day I hope to either attend overseas, or see the games in my own backyard, if Australia was a host nation.

The Perth Heat and Samsung Lions opened the series at noon on November 25, 2011 at Taichung Intercontinental Baseball Stadium. The Heat and Lions game was closer than the end score reflected. They both kept each other scoreless for the first two innings, but the Heat opened the scoring with one in the top of the third, although the Lions replied with three runs. They matched each other with one run a piece in the sixth inning, and with the score at Lions four, Heat two, it was certainly game on with three innings to go. Perth catcher Allan de San Miguel had contributed to half of the Heat's runs with a solo home run, but in the bottom of the eighth inning, the Lions ran away with the game, scoring six runs. The 10–2 final score looked like a bit of a thrashing, yet the Heat did stay with them for most of the game, but four fielding errors were quite costly and they were also out-hit, seven to twelve.

Even though the game wasn't the result I was hoping for, the players were richer for the experience and they had an opportunity to reflect on what worked and what didn't go as planned for their next game.

The Heat played the Uni-President 7-Eleven Lions on November 26, at the same venue from the previous day. Taking on another team called the Lions presented its own challenges as they had lost their opening game to the Fukuoka SoftBank Hawks 6–5. The Lions took the lead in the top of the second inning 2–1, but the Hawks scored two runs in the bottom of the third and three more in the fifth, making the score 6–2, Hawks. The Lions didn't give up, though; they scored three runs in the top of the ninth, which gave local fans plenty to cheer about. But they just fell short, losing 6–5. Therefore, the Heat and the Lions needed to win to stay in the series, and they produced one of the best games, the only game to go extra innings.

The Lions opened the scoring at the top of the sixth inning with two runs, and the Heat made it all square in the bottom of the eighth, scoring two of their own. Both teams were blanked for runs in the ninth inning and in the top of the tenth, the Lions scored a run, which the Heat couldn't match, and the Lions won 3–2. It was again fielding errors which hurt the Heat with three. To their credit they really made it count with the bat as they only had four hits to the Lions' ten, yet they managed to score two runs.

The Lions could breathe easier knowing the Hawks beat the Samsung Lions 9–0 in the noon game on November 26, and if they could beat Samsung on November 27 with a few insurance runs in hand, they could go to the final.

The Heat had a massive task to hopefully achieve their first series win against the Hawks, even though they were statistically out of the final even if they won. The Uni-President 7-Eleven Lions, however, would be pleased for them to win because the Heat's potential victory would leave three teams on two wins, this would depend on the Uni-President

7-Eleven Lions defeating Samsung, so runs scored would then decide which of the two teams played for the title.

On November 27, the Heat faced the Hawks at Taoyuan International Baseball Stadium at 1:00 p.m. Regardless of their tournament ranking, if the Heat could defeat the Hawks it would be one of their greatest wins and one for the ABL too. After giving up a run in the first inning to the Hawks, the Heat kept them off the scoreboard for the next three innings, but in the fifth the Hawks scored two, and they added another in the sixth. The final score of 4–0 was respectable considering the level of skill and power of the NPB league's best team. Three fielding errors by the Heat presented what looked like a systemic issue, with ten in three games, but they were playing overseas. They didn't have the benefit of a series of local warm-up games to become accustomed to the playing surfaces.

I hoped some players on the Heat team might turn heads from the opposition coaching staffs and players off contract or looking for a baseball challenge in Asia might attract some offers. Even though no signings were reported, it was still an opportunity to be seen. It's quite possible as more series are played that Australian players might attract interest with standout performances.

The Samsung Lions defeated the Uni-President 7-Eleven Lions 6–3, which booked Samsung's spot in the final against the Hawks on November 29. Given that the Hawks had beaten the Lions 9–0 only a few days previously, they went into the final strong favourites.

Japan and South Korea have a sporting rivalry similar to Australia and New Zealand in rugby union, and when it comes to baseball the Koreans and the Japanese have both won their share of baseball's most prestigious international tournaments. South Korea won the last Olympic gold medal for baseball at the Beijing 2008 Olympic Games, which was the last Olympics to include the sport as a medal event until at least 2020 and Japan has claimed back-to-back Baseball World Classic titles by winning the 2006 and 2009 classics.

The Hawks made the right start, scoring in the first inning and both teams were blanked for the next three innings, but in the fifth the Lions scored five, and despite the Hawks fighting back in the bottom of the eighth with two runs, the Lions put out their spark by not allowing any more runs. It was quite an occasion because for the first time in the short history of the Asia Series, the NPB league's complete dominance had been broken.

Samsung's Won-Sam Jang was the 2011 series Most Valuable Player, and when you consider that Japanese pitching ace Yu Darvish was the 2006 MVP, it is clear that the Asia Series has a chance to be one of the premier international club baseball tournaments.

The fact the ABL is represented in the series means its exposure to international baseball can grow and the players and coaching staff will only benefit from the experience.

I have been fortunate enough to meet the Perth Heat's American field manager Brooke Knight on a few occasions, and he has tremendous passion for the game and people skills which inspire. When I've seen the Heat play in the ABL, they look cohesive, the demeanour of the team always appears positive and there is a winning culture built on respect and best utilising the team's many talented players. It came as no surprise to me when they won the 2010/2011 ABL Championship Series. After that, I hoped Knight would return and pass on more of his knowhow for another season, which he did faithfully.

I asked Knight to comment on what he felt were some of the positives from playing in the 2011 Asia Series, and in an e-mail dated April 16, 2012, he shared some of his thoughts with me:

> Participating in the Asia Series was really a special privilege. There are two things in particular that I will fondly remember for years to come. First, the spirit and energy of the fans and the environment was so much different, yet uniquely special, and I know that our guys really enjoyed the opportunity to showcase what Australia has to offer the international baseball community. Second, the quality of the talent, and the way that many of these Pacific Rim countries approach the game we all love, was refreshing to see. Their passion and respect for the game was apparent during our pregame preparation, infield/outfield practice, and during the game. There was always intent, effort, and hustle, and they retained a sense of pride in ensuring all of these characteristics were an integral part of their image. It reminded me of the college game here in the US, and how so many guys are taught to play the game hard all the time, and respect it always. Refreshing to say the least.

The Perth Heat returned to the 2011/2012 ABL season with an experience no other Australian team had, making them the first-ever ABL team to stake a claim for an Asia Series title. It was a notable extra the second season of the new ABL offered. The international flavour of the league and players with Major League experience gave Australian fans the opportunity to see more great baseball on home soil.

CHAPTER 9
THE ABL 2011/2012

The second season of the new ABL approached with the headline of a misleading proposed American import player who tried to con two teams and the league. Some might say it was an unfortunate beginning, yet the Breland Brown affair proved that news of the ABL had crossed many lands and oceans. It was a desired league to play in and some people were prepared to say anything for the chance.

I first became aware in early October 2011 that American Major League outfielder Xavier Paul had reportedly signed to play with the Brisbane Bandits for the 2011/2012 season. My initial reaction was the Bandits front office had landed themselves a player with a glowing baseball resume. I assumed new field manager, American Kevin Jordan who had played in the previous ABL and had been a Major Leaguer himself, had snared a notable catch for the ABL. While Paul wasn't at that time a full-time Major Leaguer, he had played parts of seasons at that level from 2009–2011, and there weren't too many ABL positional players with similar experience. I even read an article on an Australian Baseball News Internet site where Paul was touted as an early predication for league MVP.

I saw Breland Brown's name on the Sydney Blue Sox roster around the same time; I assumed he was a minor leaguer and I hoped he would do his bit to help the Blue Sox.

Even though several American sports news services wrote about Brown after the ABL season started on November 4, 2011, it is important to note the story broke in Australia before the season began.

Brown had masqueraded as a player agent for Xavier Paul, and he used Paul as a golden bargaining chip to get his other supposed client, Breland Brown, an ABL opportunity, as it was conditional that the two were a package deal.

It was all going fine until the Bandits followed up on Paul, who hadn't arrived ahead of the season as expected. Much to the Bandits' shock, Paul and his real manager knew nothing about agreeing to play in Australia. Brown's ploy instantly lost its best trading commodity and quickly exposed his own misrepresentation. Neither player ever wore an ABL uniform or played a game, yet the event was quite a lesson.

Brown had some experience with the process of player management as he had signed some deals with affiliated teams; the most notable was his stint with the Arizona Diamondbacks organisation playing on their rookie team Missoula in 2011. He participated in eleven games and had a .171 batting average. Prior to this, during the 2009 season, he played some independent baseball in the US and had hit below .200 there. So his career numbers weren't much to work with in terms of marketability.

When it came to Paul, the ABL did carry out necessary due diligence with the Pittsburgh Pirates and they gave their approval as a club for him to play in the ABL. The Pirates selected Paul off waivers from the Los Angeles Dodgers on April 26, 2011 and he had appeared in 121 games with them. There were several other formalities the ABL carried out regarding Paul, which Brown was able to satisfy with his creativity, but his biggest break was that Paul was part of the

Pirates organisation, who have a good relationship with the ABL, having sent several minor leaguers to Australia. Brown was probably completely unaware of this factor, yet it unintentionally gave his venture some decent oxygen.

Part of me believes Brown's strategy was to try to stall the Bandits with Paul and meanwhile ensure his own passage. It could have worked had the Bandits continued to liaise with his sham agent, but they wisely inquired in the right direction and made contact with Paul's real representatives.

If Brown had played in the ABL, it wouldn't have been for long given his career numbers. Yet his chances of playing anywhere in the future seemed completely lost as his scam became international baseball news, and MLB reportedly conducted an internal investigation of the matter.

The only commonality Paul and Brown are known to have is they were both born within a few hours distance of each other in Louisiana and separated by a few months in age. Brown was born on December 12, 1984, in Marrero, and Paul was born on February 25, 1985, in Slidell.

It is possible Brown followed Paul's exploits closely as it is common for sports people to keep track of athletes from their local area or state out of interest and it can't be ruled out the two might have played some youth or high school baseball against each other. Clearly, there seems to be nothing random about Brown's selection of Paul as there were thousands of other AAA and emerging Major Leaguers he could have chosen from.

Whilst I'm certain Brown was an unwelcome and uncomfortable topic for season two of the ABL, his wheeling and dealing did give local and overseas fans something extra to talk about. The incident has tightened regulation and conditions for foreign players who wish to participate in the league, so in the end all Brown did was make it harder for fraudsters to try the same trickery.

Brown was quickly forgotten as the new season revealed numerous enhancements. Season two certainly gave fans and players more. The regular season was increased from forty games to forty-five, the first two stages of the postseason (the semi-final series and preliminary final series) became best of five games although the Championship Series remained best of three, the Asia Series was included and an ABL All-Star game was added, pitting a team consisting of imports versus the best available local talent as a Team Australia.

James Beresford played twelve games for the Melbourne Aces during the latter stages of the previous season. Since 2007, I've followed his professional career closely but hadn't seen him play and I hoped at long last I would get the chance. The Minnesota Twins prospect accumulated a .404 batting average during his ABL stint. The talented shortstop or second baseman also recorded a hit off Cuban flamethrower pitcher Aroldis Chapman during the 2009 World Baseball Classic, a task that some of Beresford's teammates with MLB experience hadn't been able to match. As the Blue Sox opened their season at home against the Aces, on November 4, I hoped Beresford would be on their roster, but unfortunately some minor off-season surgery ruled him out for the ABL season while he recuperated. All went successfully because Beresford opened the 2012 minor league season a level higher from the previous year with the Twins AA team, the New Britain Rock Cats.

The Blue Sox did well in their opening series, winning three of their four games, yet it was seventeen-year-old Aces left-handed pitcher Daniel McGrath who became a topic of discussion during a chat I had with Ulli Wermuth on

Sunday, November 6, 2011. I had come to know Ulli, who is German, through the Manly Eagles Sydney Major League club, and he was holidaying in Australia for part of the summer and playing some baseball. We were at Manly's home field, Aquatic Reserve, as a quick but heavy downfall of rain halted the afternoon game. With a washout looming, we talked some ABL back at the clubhouse and as a baseball scout, player, and coach, Ulli knew what a super prospect looked like.

"Daniel McGrath for the Aces is a talent," said Ulli with the same certainty as a university professor discussing an award-winning research thesis. "His pitching speed for his age, size, and overall makeup is high calibre." At 1.91 metres in height, McGrath was a tall teenager, and at ninety-three kilograms he was solid too. Baseball likes its imperial unit measurements, particularly for gauging speed, and McGrath's pitches were getting clocked at 93 mph.

Interestingly, McGrath had debuted for the Aces during the previous ABL season, which meant he would have been sixteen years old. He appeared in four games, pitching 9.1 innings with an ERA of 3.86. For 2011/2012, he appeared in thirteen games, pitching 10.2 innings.

Ulli was spot on regarding McGrath, as he joined the Boston Red Sox organisation for reportedly a $400,000 sign-on bonus on February 8, 2012. A pleasing detail is he always dreamed to play for the Red Sox, and his American-born mother is a staunch Red Sox fan. McGrath's signing was picked up by mainstream news services and the *Sydney Morning Herald* featured an article on him dated February 9, 2012, titled "Off to the diamond life: teen signs for Sox," written by Stathi Paxinos, and Network Ten's Evening News did a sports piece on him. A baseball story in the mass media reaches millions of Australians and encourages people to think more about the sport.

It was the same media coverage when Aussies Damian Moss and Glenn Williams signed with the Atlanta Braves in the early 1990s, which helped fuel my baseball appetite and desire to be just like them. McGrath has no doubt inspired others too.

On Saturday, November 19, 2011 I attended the Sydney Blue Sox versus Perth Heat evening game. Graeme Lloyd was on the Heat's coaching staff, and after the game I had a chance to chat with him under the main grandstand. At two metres tall, eighteen centimetres separates us in height. When I met him as a fourteen-year-old on the Queensland Gold Coast in early 1994, he towered over me like a giant. Despite many years, I was again looking up to Lloyd.

The return of the ABL presented a chance to be face-to-face with one of my greatest baseball heroes, and as he had taken some time out during the previous summer season too, it was my first chance to see him again.

Lloyd exudes a natural affection that is conveyed with a warm grin and a comfortable demeanour.

"Hello, Graeme. In June, I missed you by one day in New York. I was at a Yankees game the day after you played in an old-timers game, but I don't think you're an old-timer."

He laughed and said, "I am an old-timer."

I had a copy of, *Boomerang Baseball*, to give to him. "I wrote this book and you're mentioned in it quite a few times. That was absolutely amazing what you did during the 1996 World Series, so I've written about it."

He took a moment to glace at the book and read over the back cover description. "Thank you, Nicholas, I really appreciate this." The warmth and gratitude in his voice made every hour I put into the book well worth it. To be able to give Lloyd something after all the inspiration and wonderful memories he gave me and many other people made my week. He shook my hand, and I knew then and there that moment was the highlight of the season for me.

With the Heat in Sydney, I took the opportunity to catch up with some of the other players and coaches. Field manager Brooke Knight was walking past as I finished talking with Lloyd who recognised me straight away, which was a buzz.

"Thank you for coming back for another season of ABL, your commitment to the sport here is making a valuable contribution," I said.

"Thank you for the kind words." The Heat had a strong series against the Blue Sox, winning all four games, including two they won by over ten runs. On Sunday, November 20, 2011 they beat the Blue Sox 19–3. Five days later, they played their first game in the Asia Series.

On November 19 Heat catcher Allan de San Miguel spotted me standing near the visitors' dugout entrance to the field, and as he walked toward me he asked cheerfully, "Hey, how you doing?" and we shook hands.

"I'm well, how about you?"

De San Miguel said, "Pretty good, I'm pleased this season is here having spent a fair bit of the US season on the DL." How baseball players cope on the disabled list when someone else is eager to fill their spot is a real mind game, which must take real discipline to not become too distracted, but de San Miguel always seemed to have a smile on his face.

"Well, you're looking fit as a fiddle."

"Thanks, mate."

Mathew Kennelly was sitting near the dugout steps, and I gave him a wave. He waved back, so I walked over to him.

"Well done on getting a run in AAA this year," I said. Having spent the majority of his 2011 season in AA, Kennelly played two games for the Braves AAA team Gwinnett. He had seven at-bats and collected two hits, and at twenty-two years old he had demonstrated he could hit AAA pitchers with Major League experience.

"Thank you," he replied.

"What was it like?"

"It was good to be able to catch for guys with Big League time behind them and face pitchers who have been up there helps you know what to expect."

Even though Kennelly is a minor league catcher, for the Heat he often plays corner outfield positions, third and first base, he catches some games, and also fills the role of designated hitter at times. With three notable minor league catchers to choose from, the Heat are able to rotate their backstops. Kennelly certainly brings a lot to the team and his consistency with the bat is impressive. During the 2010/2011 ABL season, he finished the regular season with a .306 batting average and .297 for the 2011/2012 regular season.

When it comes to baseballers from Western Australia, where there is one Kennelly, another is nearby. Sure enough, Tim came out of the dugout, saying, "Hey Nick, how you doing?" After so many seasons in the US, Tim has a hint of an American accent. "We seem to be seeing a lot of each other," he said as we both laughed. I was amazed after spending the better part of eight months over there and heading right into another season of baseball with the ABL, Tim had such a spring in his step. That energy sure did a lot for him because he finished the 2011/2012 season as the league's MVP/Helms Award winner.

Based on my assessment of Kennelly's season, he contributed in so many different ways, at such a high standard, that league MVP was a well deserved recognition. He was a leader on a team which finished the regular season in first place, thirteen wins ahead of the next team, with a winning percentage of .756. He led the league in runs batted in with thirty-nine and his .374 batting average was further confirmation of his reliability with the bat.

During the 2012 minor league season, he was promoted to the Phillies' AAA team Lehigh Valley, and he crushed a home run in his first game at that level, which was quite an impression to make on field manager and Hall of Famer Ryne Sandberg. Kennelly spent most of the season at AA Reading, but change was in the air as his fastball was frequently clocked at 95 mph. From about the second half of the 2012 minor league season, Kennelly appeared for Reading as a relief pitcher, then a decision was made to continue his baseball journey within the Phillies organisation as a pitcher.

It is often said in baseball a lot can happen in one year, and when it came to the ABL, one player in particular made immense progress. Heat pitcher Warwick Saupold put together mediocre numbers during the 2010/2011 regular season with three wins and two losses, an ERA of 5.52, he threw 44 innings, he struck out 41 batters and his WHIP was 1.50. Those were okay enough numbers, but by the end of the 2011/2012 regular season, his overall numbers were the best in the league, with five wins and three losses, an ERA of 1.41, 70 innings pitched, 53 batters struck out, and his WHIP was 0.93. On January 16, 2012, he turned twenty-two and before the season had ended he signed a professional contract with the Detroit Tigers organisation. Saupold had bucked a trend by inking a deal in his early twenties, when most players signed from Australia without previous minor league experience were almost always teenagers.

Saupold began the 2012 minor league season with the Tigers A ball team West Michigan. It was still quite cool in the Midwest in April as he had come from a hot Australian summer and the US climate did take some getting used to because at first he was a little inconsistent. But after pitching 58 innings mostly as a reliever, he had two wins and one loss, an ERA of 2.79, struck out 58 batters and his WHIP was 1.172. Just after the halfway point of the season, he was promoted to the Tigers high A ball team Lakeland and after three innings of work he hadn't conceded a run.

It was inspiring to see Saupold make so much progress and I hope his career has no limits in terms of the opportunities which may be presented to him. I couldn't help wonder what had contributed to him refining his skills to such a level, as he obviously had aptitude, but it seemed he'd found the right dynamics and was continuing to develop with every challenge. Who better to answer this question than the Perth Heat's coaching staff. Coach and Player Development Manager Steve Fish kindly shared his thoughts with me in his e-mail dated April 12, 2012, which comments on Saupold across both ABL seasons:

> Warwick busted his tail to get into shape to crack the starting rotation with the Heat. He started out as our #4–5 and his velocity quickly jumped a good 5 mph once he started getting quality innings. By mid-January, he showed us that he could be a #1 on any rotation in the league. He is also the best athlete of any pitcher I saw in the ABL this year and his ability to field his position saved him in several key situations.

The Heat's Chairman of the Board Geoff Hooker also offered some valuable insights, particularly into Saupold's 2011/2012 growth, in his e-mail to me dated April 11, 2012:

> We were delighted when the Tigers signed Saupold. It represents what the Perth Heat and the Baseball WA High Performance Program are all about. Our program is strongly supported by Baseball WA and the WA State Government because it is a pathway mechanism for our elite players. The success and subsequent signing of Saupold shows that the ABL, with the support of its underpinning high-performance programs, can deliver players direct into the full season of a MLB minor league system. It's a major step forward for the Heat and Baseball WA.
>
> That said, the ABL is a highly competitive league. Alone, it is not a "pathway" league. Rather, a highly competitive environment where the best players from within the Baseball WA High Performance Program and other states get an opportunity to prove themselves.
>
> The success of Saupold at ABL level is a true testament to the ability and character of this young man. He stepped up this year and was a key player on a championship team, proving consistently that he could get Major League calibre hitters out, many times in tough situations.

While the 2010/2011 season presented prospects and players with Major League experience, the 2011/2012 season brought with it a new lot Saupold also tested his pitching skills against, and in the case of opposing pitchers with Major League experience, by season's end he had confirmed himself as the ace of the league.

The 2011/2012 season had several import players who were on their way to the Majors or had already been there, which gave fans a chance to see players of this standard on their team or playing within the league. There were also several Australians who fitted this profile.

Taiwanese middle-infielder Chin-lung Hu was on the Adelaide Bite's team and at twenty-seven years old, he was still very much in the prime of his career. Hu made his Major League debut with the Los Angeles Dodgers on September 1, 2007 and wore Dodger Blue from 2007–2010, and played for the New York Mets in 2011. The alumni of Taiwan-born players with Major League experience continues to grow, with Chien-Ming Wang, Chin-Feng Chen, Hong-Chih Kuo, Fu-Te Ni, Wei-Yin Chen, and Chin-hui Tsao all having played at that level. Hu's participation in the ABL drew attention to the league from adoring Taiwanese fans who closely monitored his progress and spectators in Australia who were able to see him play on Aussie soil. Hu played 28 games in the ABL and had a .277 batting average with three home runs. His final game for the 2011/2012 season was on December 31, 2011, to recover from a minor injury. He was signed as a free agent by the Cleveland Indians on January 11, 2012, but the Indians released him on April 1, 2012. He was picked up by American independent ball team Southern Maryland for the 2012 season. Having Hu in the ABL further displayed the international breadth of the league and calibre of players it attracted.

Jason Hirsh, a 2.03-metre tall American pitcher, had Big League experience with the Houston Astros and Colorado

Rockies and suited up for the Melbourne Aces. Hirsh had made his Major League debut with the Astros on August 12, 2006 and spent parts of the 2007 and 2008 season with the Rockies. He was still in the Rockies organisation in 2009 and in 2010 was part of the Yankees organisation. Injury cost him all of his 2011 US season and the ABL was an opportunity for him to get back on the mound following his recovery.

Hirsh participated in eight ABL games from November 13, 2011 to January 14, 2012, all pitching starts, and his numbers should take into consideration his home field was the Melbourne Showgrounds, a hitter's paradise with several short dimensions. He had two wins and two losses with an ERA of 6.90, pitching 30 innings and striking out 20 batters. I didn't manage to see Hirsh pitch as his first game was on November 13, 2011, a week after the Aces series in Sydney, but was certainly pleased he participated in the league.

I couldn't believe it when I attended a Blue Sox home series against the Adelaide Bite on January 14, 2012, and spotted number thirty-two, Ahearne, warming up in the bullpen. I looked carefully and immediately concluded it was none other than Pat Ahearne. He and many others might not have known it at the time, but the following night he was going to make history as the first American with Major League experience to participate in both versions of the ABL. Back in the ABL, he was forty-two years old, but looked at least five years younger than his actual age, and he appeared fit, with a trim and toned 1.91 metre frame.

Ahearne had joined the Bite late in the season as they had some injuries to rostered players and changes to the availability of some import players. It's a credit to Ahearne he made himself available at such short notice because it was well into the off-season, meaning he had to hit the ground running. As a player with sixteen years of minor league baseball service, including time in independent baseball, Ahearne was no stranger to having a bag always packed and preparing his mind and body for a challenge on the baseball field.

I met him a few times during the previous ABL and he's what I call California Cool, with a relaxed timbre to his accent and the Golden State glow to his skin. He was born in San Francisco on December 10, 1969 and attended Pepperdine University in Malibu, California. Toward the end of the 1998/1999 season, when he played with the Perth Heat, I saw him at the newly built Sydney Olympic Park Complex in Homebush he looked like he had spent the day enjoying the beach or harbour as he wore a straw hat, board shorts and a light short-sleeve shirt. Drafted by the Detroit Tigers in the seventh round of the 1992 amateur draft, I'm sure Ahearne's baseball journey has taken him many places, with lots of memories to cherish forever.

He had three stints in the previous ABL, which was due somewhat to teams having a set affiliation with MLB clubs and as Ahearne changed organisations in the US, this to an extent dictated the ABL teams he could play for. From 1996–1999, he played within the Dodgers, Mets, and Mariners organisations, in addition to some independent ball teams. The first ABL club he played for was the Adelaide Giants in 1996/1997, followed by the Melbourne Reds in 1997/1998, and the Perth Heat in 1998/1999. He was the ace on the Reds 1997/1998 ABL Championship Series–winning team. His regular season statistics with the Heat in 1998/1999 handed him the ABL Pitcher of the Year Award, with seven wins and three losses, an ERA of 2.16, throwing 87.1 innings, and 72 strikeouts. He achieved this on a Heat team which was uncharacteristically weak as the previous ABL started to show clear signs of wavering.

Ahearne was a rare American to join the previous ABL with Big League experience, as most organisations affiliated to ABL clubs sent prospects. He made his Major League debut with the Detroit Tigers on June 14, 1995, and played his final game at that level on June 30, 1995. He pitched in four games, including three starts, with two losses, an ERA of 11.70, pitching ten innings and struck out four batters. It's not uncommon for pitchers to start their MLB careers with numbers which are somewhat elevated as they adjust to the Majors.

Having Ahearne back in the ABL confirmed the lifelong friendships baseball players from all over the world establish by playing the game they love and his steadfast desire to take the pitcher's mound.

He made two appearances in the ABL regular season and both were pitching starts. I saw his first game on January 15, 2012, in Sydney. His first two innings looked sharp, keeping the batters quiet, but by his fourth inning, it seemed the batters had a better read of him and he was tapped around a bit. He came out of the game after 4.2 innings, yet with such a limited preparation and plenty of jetlag still in his system, I feel he pitched well. He took the loss, with an ERA of 9.64, and gave up five earned runs. His numbers were similar during his next start against the Bandits in Brisbane on January 22, 2012. However, without a preseason and most of the regular season, it was a very hard job and to his credit he gave it a go.

I had an opportunity to speak with him after the game, in Adelaide's dugout, on January 15. "Pat, it's great to see you back in the ABL!" I think I took him a bit by surprise because the team was clearing out the dugout, players were signing autographs and he was just taking a moment to reflect on the game. "Thank you," he replied with an appreciative grin. He added, "I only just flew in, but it's good to be here."

"So what do you think of this version of the ABL?" I asked.

"The standard is definitely higher and all the players are using wood bats, which is good." For most of the duration of the previous ABL, players who were contracted to play in the US minors or Majors had to use timber, those who weren't could use steel bats. A young kid was standing waiting to get Ahearne to sign his ball and I said to the boy, "This man has played in the Majors with the Detroit Tigers," and all of a sudden fans seeking autographs turned on Ahearne in a drove. "Welcome back Pat," I said. As we shook hands, he said, "Thanks, I appreciate it."

The Perth Heat also picked up a player with Major League experience late in the season. Pitcher Virgil Vasquez also from California, was born and grew up in Santa Barbara. Like Ahearne, he debuted with the Detroit Tigers. Vasquez debuted on May 13, 2007, appearing in five games, including three pitching starts. He also played for the Pittsburgh Pirates in 2009, where he appeared in 14 games and threw 44.2 innings. His last game in the Majors was on October 4, 2009; he spent the 2010 season playing in the minors for the Tampa Bay Rays organisation and in 2011 he played the season with independent ball team Southern Maryland.

Vasquez instantly dazzled in the ABL. His only two regular season games were both starts on January 14 and January 20, 2012. Both games were no-decisions, but his ERA combined to be 1.64, pitching eleven innings. He took his sharp form into the ABL postseason and was awarded the

Championship Series Most Valuable Player as the Heat made it back-to-back titles.

Kevin Jordan's return to the ABL as the Brisbane Bandits field manager was further proof of the great friendships and personal connections to Australia several American imports had developed during stints in the previous ABL. By the time of the second ABL, Jordan had established himself in the coaching ranks of the Philadelphia Phillies farm system, which meant he brought coaching expertise and Major League playing experience. Like the Bandits General Manager Paul Gonzalez, Jordan fell in love and married an Australian, which worked out well for baseball in Australia because it meant both of these players would be part of our game for years to come. Jordan played two seasons in the previous ABL and his .390 batting average with the Bandits in 1992/1993 confirmed him as a class act.

He played his entire Major League career with the Phillies from 1995–2001, making his debut on August 8, 1995 and playing his final game at that level on October 7, 2001. As an infielder, he did his job playing either first, second, or third base and often called upon to pinch hit.

I found it pleasing to continually see remnants of the previous ABL helping the new league, with past players wanting to do their bit to contribute to the future of the game in Australia.

As I attended most of the Blue Sox 2011/2012 home games, I was fortunate to see two American imports on the Blue Sox team play regularly. Lubbock, Texas–born outfielder Tyler Collins hardly missed a game of the regular season, playing in forty-three. With a year of minor league baseball behind him, he showed a lot of maturity on the field and with the bat. He played for the World All-Stars against

Team Australia in the inaugural ABL All-Star Game and it was his home run which put the game out of reach, earning him Most Valuable Player honours with the final score 8–5, World All-Stars.

He had a knack for clubbing multihit games and on January 15 and January 19, 2012, he had three hits from four at-bats in both games. He finished the season with a .298 batting average and three home runs.

Houston Astros outfield prospect American Brandon Barnes was a gift to the ABL and the Blue Sox. Having split his 2011 season between the Astros AA and AAA teams, Barnes was the rock who helped the Blue Sox bats boom, as they got off to a slow start in the batter's box. Barnes joined the team a few weeks into the season, participating in twenty-nine games. His .322 batting average and six home runs made him a crowd favourite. Barnes attended the Astros 2012 Major League spring training and his bat boomed playing AAA with Oklahoma City, keeping his average close to .350 well into the season. His excellent performance was rewarded when he made his Major League debut for the Astros on August 7, 2012.

It was a personal highlight, seeing Brad Thomas pitch for the Blue Sox. After a solid 2010 season with the Detroit Tigers, he rested for the 2010/2011 ABL season, but he attended some series as a VIP spectator, and much to my surprise he instantly recognised me when he was walking under the main grandstand. I'd sent him a copy of *Boomerang Baseball* during his 2010 season, which he confirmed receiving. The author photograph on the back cover had done its job. Thomas said, "At first I thought it was some kind of a joke. Because there is a sports writer named Lynn Henning who covers the Tigers and I thought he was messing around with me when the copy was delivered to my locker."

Aussie Major League pitcher Grant Balfour had said something similar when *The American Dream: From Perth to Sacramento* was placed on his locker chair with the surfer and kangaroo imagery on the front cover.

The year 2011 had been a frustrating year with the Tigers for Thomas, as injury cost him most of the season. His participation in the 2011/2012 ABL season was his return to the mound following arm surgery and making a full recovery. He pitched in five games for the Blue Sox during the regular season, and four were starts. He had one win and one loss, with an ERA of 2.42, over 22.1 innings pitched, with 13 strikeouts.

He made Australian baseball history when he joined the Brother Elephants in Taiwan's Chinese Professional Baseball League for the 2012 season, as he became the first Australian to play MLB and participate in NPB, the KBO, and the CPBL.

By the end of the 2011/2012 ABL regular season, the Perth Heat finished thirteen wins ahead of the second placed Melbourne Aces, this confirmed the Heat as the team to beat in the playoffs, yet the Aces were only one win in front of the rest of the field, who were all even on twenty wins and twenty-five losses. Adelaide, Sydney, Brisbane, and Canberra's seasons weren't fully determined until the last regular season games concluded for each of these teams. Proof of the competitiveness of the ABL was how close the regular season had been and Canberra was in second place going into the last round but found itself at the bottom of the table because the jam of teams was so tight. In assessing the regular season, it was clear the ABL was a good product for the fans, players and the sport. As was the case in season one, the teams placing fifth and sixth didn't progress to the postseason, meaning that Perth, Sydney, Adelaide, and Melbourne all went through.

Fans received an extra treat for the 2011/2012 season, with the first two stages (semi-final series and preliminary final series) of the postseason increasing from a three-game series to a five-game series. It was a big test for the final four teams, which advanced to the playoffs as they had to stretch their resources to the limit, knowing if they made it to the Championship Series they could plan for the smaller three-game series.

Fox Sports again provided coverage in Australia, but the second season brought expanded television coverage for the postseason finals, Championship Series, and All-Star Game. This was a significant advancement for baseball in Australia because never before had either version of the ABL been televised so internationally, which included ESPN Star Sports carrying it in Asia and the MLB Network in North America. Technology has become much more global since the previous ABL. I received e-mails from friends in America advising me they had watched ABL postseason games on MLB Network. Chris Vaccaro was quick to tell me, "I saw some of that ABL Championship Series and it looked good, way better than I was expecting." It was fantastic to see an Australian brand of baseball reaching fans in all the baseball hot spots of the world, as well as growing markets like India and China.

The Adelaide Bite and Sydney Blue Sox were both bundled out of the postseason, which put the Heat up against the Aces and the Championship Series was hosted by Perth. The fact the series went to three games as it did during the previous season was further evidence of the competitiveness of the ABL. The Heat won game one on February 10, 2012, defeating the Aces 4–1. The Aces bounced back in game two on February 11, winning 3–2, and game three on February 12 was a thriller and a test of endurance, lasting thirteen innings, with the Heat winning 7–6, making it back-to-back championships. The Heat's Coach and Player Development Manager Steve Fish provided a special insight regarding the team in his e-mail to me dated April 12, 2012:

> The chemistry that made up this squad was one of a kind. These guys have played together for so long and are roughly the same age and played juniors together. We had a crop of quality local AA- and AAA-calibre players mixed with a bit of MLB experience and a few American imports that figured things out pretty quickly. Our staff was readily available at any time and worked extremely well together, and were on board with each and every decision made throughout the entire season. It was a pretty close knit group and Brooke did an excellent job of sewing loose ends when opportunities were lost, or when things began to fall apart. 2011–12 was a dream season.

Travis Blackley was the starting pitcher for the Aces in game one, on February 10 of the Championship Series, going head to head with the Heat's Virgil Vasquez. Vasquez took the win, yet there was a major result for Blackley and additional testimony of the global reach of the ABL as he was signed by the San Francisco Giants as a free agent on February 16, 2012. Blackley started the year with the Giants AAA team Fresno, where he dominated on the mound with three wins and no losses, and an ERA of 0.39, throwing 23.1 innings. The Giants promoted him to the Majors, where he appeared in four games, with an ERA of 9.00 from five innings pitched. He was sent back down to AAA, but Oakland A's General Manager Billy Beane played some clever *Moneyball* and the A's claimed Blackley on waivers on May 15, 2012.

The A's had a very Aussie flavour before Blackley joined, with Australian pitchers Grant Balfour, Richard Thompson, and infielder Luke Hughes all appearing on the Major League roster briefly at the same time in 2012. Balfour was one of the A's most experienced relief pitchers, but Blackley joined the team having last won a game at the Major League level whilst pitching for the Seattle Mariners in 2004 and his role would be whatever he made of it.

Four Australians appearing on one MLB team in a season established a new Aussie record, yet Blackley became an inspiration and worked his way into the starting rotation. On June 15, 2012, he started against the San Diego Padres and pitched six innings for two earned runs, which gave him his first MLB win since 2004. He had a massive job in front of him when he started against the Los Angeles Dodgers on June 21, as the Dodgers started Clayton Kershaw, the National League's 2011 Cy Young Award winner and pitching Triple Crown winner. Facing a pitcher who led the National League during the previous season in wins, ERA, and strikeouts was a challenge Blackley stepped up to. He pitched eight innings for one earned run in a no-decision, but in a game the A's would win. On July 1, he started against the power-hitting Texas Rangers and threw seven innings for one earned run and another win.

The year 2012 was a season in which all of Travis Blackley's talent and potential came together, and the long road he had travelled, including stops in Mexico, South Korea, and Australia, finally brought him back to the apex of baseball, where he pitched on one of the most effective staffs in MLB and he quickly became a good news story for A's fans and all his supporters in Australia and across the world.

It was remarkable to reflect that he pitched in game one of the ABL Championship Series on February 10 and just over four months later he earned his second career Major League win, on June 15. Blackley is a great story that I hope has many more volumes to it.

It looked natural seeing Blackley and three other Australians in Oakland's green, yellow, and white, and a cap with the letter A on the front, which is all consistent with Australia's national sporting colours.

The 2011/2012 ABL season further displayed baseball in Australia is fertile ground for the growth of the sport and a place to see quality players take the field. It was a wonderful bonus to see Australian baseball history unfold so quickly into the 2012 MLB season, especially with the Oakland A's, which contributed to creating greater awareness of Australia's involvement in the game.

It is the business of baseball in Australia where the sport must work hard to continue to win the hearts and minds of new local fans and nurture Aussie baseball talent with cutting-edge development programs and a competitive national competition.

CHAPTER 10
THE BUSINESS OF BASEBALL IN AUSTRALIA

The Australian sporting landscape and the domestic business market are unique; both require careful research and assessment for any local or international product to survive and succeed. What works in one overseas market doesn't always transfer to Australia and this is true of sport and even consumables.

The ABL's previous venture, which spanned from 1989/1990 to 1998/1999, often cited as baseball's golden age in Australia is also testimony of its inability to survive as a national competition. The reasons for the first ABL's demise consist of many factors, yet financial instability in terms of attracting sponsors and creating stable revenue both presented considerable barriers. There was also a lack of uniformity with regards to the business management of league teams and this led to clubs folding. The league itself was shut down in late 1999 due to substantial debts.

Yet the previous venture which survived for a decade gave baseball in Australia an opportunity to develop the best possible plan to make the new ABL venture viable and sustainable. If mission statements could be condensed to one word, "sustainability" underpins the ABL's future and the further growth of the sport in Australia.

While the ABL had its own history as one way to assist the development of the new league, the sporting and business environment of the ten years occurring after the previous venture was stacked with case studies of stumbled and failed sports leagues in Australia, as well as unsuccessful consumables, which indicated that the ABL's previous demise wasn't an isolated incident, but one of a list of sports and products which had found Australia a tough market to crack. Therefore, multiple non-baseball experiments could also help expose pitfalls baseball might wish to take close note of, and even though consumables may not seem to have an obvious relationship with sport, it's important to consider both as products.

When news of the new ABL was made public in 2009, a combination of emotions swept over me. I was thrilled it was finally returning, but also very fearful because other sports with much bigger profiles and participation rates than baseball had all taken significant hits during the ABL's absence. In some ways, I felt baseball was taking a big risk, yet the chance to try it again had returned and there was no doubt in my mind administrators of the sport were determined to work toward sustainability.

Despite this, the road of enhancing and developing new sports leagues in Australia was so recently littered with some ugly crashes that I found myself trying to dissect these failed ventures to identify what free education the ABL could attain and learn from.

Rugby union is a top tier sport in Australia, with a solid following of the national team, the Wallabies and the Southern Hemisphere competition Super Rugby. The last frontier for rugby union has been to develop a fully professional Australian national competition, much like New Zealand's

ITM Cup and South Africa's Currie Cup. In 2006 the Australian Rugby Championship (ARC) was founded with the inaugural season in 2007.

A basic business plan usually expects the first year of operation to incur a low profit or a loss, yet when the ARC sustained a reported $4.7 AUD million dollar loss, its parent body, the Australian Rugby Union (ARU), didn't proceed with a second season.

I was completely shocked by this, as rugby union is famous for its corporate image, with business CEOs, doctors, and people high on the social hierarchy sitting on their boards and employed in positions within the ARU. If any sport seemed to have the business side of things well covered, it was rugby union.

The only logical conclusion seemed to be the ARC had performed well below business expectations and the ARU couldn't see performance improving quickly enough to warrant further investment. It was a rare occasion where rugby union appeared to have failed, and for some, the demise of the ARC sent a negative message regarding the ARU's vision to provide a local fully professional league.

It became obvious the ABL had a great partnership with MLB and the Australian Baseball Federation, which many sports in Australia can't match.

The fact MLB helped underwrite the ABL gave the sport the best possible chance to eventually work toward self-managed sustainability, which was part of the ABL's strategic planning.

One of the scariest words in Australian sport is "expansion." All sports codes have tried and few have succeeded. During the previous ABL, unconvincing results were achieved attempting to expand the number of teams, so suggestions of plans to expand this version of the ABL with more local teams is challenging. Still, I'm in favour of a New Zealand–based team and or teams made up exclusively of overseas players based in Australia. My main concern is not having enough quality local players to fill the rosters of more teams, even with the inclusion of imports, and therefore potentially reducing the standard of the league.

Domestic expansion is a seductive temptress which seems to leave just about every sport in Australia with a sore or broken heart. Despite this heartache, there appears to be an incurable habit of sports trying it over and again, often with the promise that mistakes of the past have been rectified and a reliable business plan is in place. These are not quite the words of an ex-lover asking for a second chance, yet there seems to be consistency with a gloomy outcome the end result.

The National Rugby League (NRL) is a tier one Australian sport, but moves to rationalise the NRL in the late 1990s led to many bitter tears as foundation clubs established in 1908 were forced to merge, as were numerous other teams, and some teams became extinct. This was within four years of a rugby league civil war which resulted in two leagues in 1997. Part of the reasoning for rationalisation was the standard of the league suffered with new clubs, and financially the league needed to reduce in size because the NRL wasn't able to develop adequate financial goals. Yet three new teams were added to the league in 1988 and four in 1995, by 1997 all the talk was about downsizing. It was frustrating for fans to see such drastic changes, and some lost interest in rugby league as a result.

The lesson the ABL could take from the NRL's expansion attempt was the fact even a tier one sport, with high

Australian television ratings and ability to generate revenue, had taken an about-face on becoming bigger by entering new markets.

Aussie Rules Football governing body the Australian Football League (AFL) has taken a more conservative approach. In recent years the AFL added a team on the Queensland Gold Coast and a second team in Sydney. One facet of the AFL's business planning is the strategy to work in terms of decades when setting business goals for new teams, this is nice if you have deep enough pockets to plan on such a long time scale.

The ABL could certainly benefit from paying close attention to some of the AFL's strategies, yet the AFL has a tremendously strong domestic market presence and a sporting history of over one hundred years. A newcomer like the ABL can't put itself on the same frequency as the AFL because the AFL has had so long to embed itself within Australian sporting culture, which is much the same with the NRL. The ABL isn't out to compete with these sports, but both present recent examples of expansion, with the NRL achieving very mixed results and the AFL projecting losses for several years for its new teams.

Australia's highest soccer competition, the A-League, is a code the ABL should pay particularly close attention to as it takes place over Australia's summer, which is also when the ABL is played. The A-League was founded in 2004 and had its first season in 2005/2006. In less than six years of operating, it added three new teams, one of which replaced a foundation team. But two of the new clubs folded. The A-League can be considered a tier two sport and, despite having notable participation rates in schools and with local sports clubs, it is still trying to gain further popularity and momentum. It is also a relatively new league and a sport Australians haven't yet fully embraced, compared to tier one sports.

I'm one of a throng of people who feel the A-League is taking too many risks in the Australian summer sports market, which is dominated by domestic and international cricket—even as Australia's premier tier one summer sport, cricket, has experienced its own downturns in terms of crowd attendances and television ratings. Yet cricket is deeply woven into Australia's cultural identity and while it may experience a slump, its ability to recover is superior to many other Australian sports.

Subsequently, all Australian sports that participate in the summer market, and this also includes Australia's National Basketball League (NBL), most likely know they will never dethrone cricket. Despite this, the A-League seems unhindered with expansion plans: adding another team in Sydney and other locations have been mentioned, but its overdrive trial-and-error approach seems to hand the ABL free tips on what not to do when attempting to grow a sport in Australia.

The NBL is another tier two sport which has experienced its own growing pains, and there were many people in the 1990s who likened the previous ABL's growth potential to the NBL's golden years of the late 1980s and early 1990s, as both operated side by side as American sports which had captured interest in Australia with professional leagues.

Played in schools and local sports clubs, basketball has made a mark in Australia, yet it has always been in the shadow of more traditional sports, which keeps the NBL in a tier two band.

During the late 1980s and early 1990s, baseball and basketball in Australia both received considerable fuel from the biggest shift toward interest in American popular culture since World War II. In what can be described as a social phenomenon, all things American, including sport, music, clothing, and much more, did a roaring trade in Australia for over five years. This not surprisingly coincided with some of the NBL's and previous ABL's best years.

One achievement baseball made during the 1990s was crowd attendances of over ten thousand, but this statistic is at times not used correctly, as in most cases these crowds were recorded during the ABL postseason. I have occasionally read and heard this number unintentionally inferred as regular season crowd averages, which was never the case.

This is an important detail because there are people who question why the new ABL hasn't had crowds of ten thousand or more people, and what they often don't realise is Australia was in the midst of an American social phenomenon. Also, the current venues don't seat that many people and some of the past ABL facilities were rectangular fields used and designed for other sporting codes, which had substantial seating capacity.

This version of the ABL doesn't have a social phenomenon giving it extra momentum, but this is a good thing because the boom of the late 1980s and early 1990s was followed by a crash. This time around, the ABL may achieve slower, short-term growth. However, it is likely to lead to more sustainable, medium- and long-term advancement because there isn't an unsustainable craze causing short-term inflated popularity.

Introducing new consumables such as fast foods has also seen a trend of new players experiencing difficulties in the Australian market and when individual cases are assessed these can be helpful to the ABL.

Too often I'm left guessing as to what market research was considered before carrying out some ventures. Restaurant chain Boston Market had a short go in Sydney during the early 2000s and quickly found it hard going. It was a good enough idea to offer home-style roasted meals, as fast food in Australia usually has a fried, pizza, or burger theme to it, but having had one of their meals it was instantly obvious to me that Boston Market had priced itself out of the market. The product was decent, but Returned Servicemen Clubs and various Sports Leagues Clubs offered budget roast meals. It was far cheaper to have a roast meal at a leagues club.

The lesson for the ABL when considering Boston Market is to carefully price tickets to games and merchandise and be aware of competitor pricing such as the NBL, and the A-League. Cricket is a market leader unlikely to ever be threatened by any other summer sports. The ABL, NBL, and A-League are all trying to carve a profitable and permanent place for themselves in Australia's summer sports calendar and each has its own challenges.

There are some rumblings from a few ABL fans that ticket prices should be lower, and counter-arguments are the prices are cheaper than NRL tickets. This is a flawed argument because the NRL is a winter sport with a firm position in the market. Also, the NRL has a much more established demand and market presence, and this makes pitting ABL ticket costs alongside the NRL's irrelevant.

It's reasonable to make some comparisons between ABL ticket prices and those charged by the NBL or A-League, as value for money across these three sports should be highly competitive.

The ABL has a treasure trove when it comes to merchandise, as it has New Era as a licenced supplier for baseball caps and Majestic as the licenced supplier for uniforms and supporter apparel, which is the same as its MLB cousin. The NBL would no doubt like to have the same brands as the NBA and the A-League with the English Premier League. The ABL enjoys something of merchandising edge.

Taco Bell fast food has a longer history in Australia than is often realised. They originally made an entry in the early 1980s, but were challenged by a local restaurant with a similar name and were subsequently unable to trade under the Taco Bell brand name. Their biggest drive in Australia came in the late 1990s, but by the mid-2000s they had withdrawn completely from the Australian market.

Taco Bell is a case study the ABL can consider in terms of why it is essential to know your market and meet or exceed expectations. I had a meal at the George Street, Sydney, store in 1999; as someone famous for burning two-minute noodles, my skills in the kitchen are at a beginner level on a good day. Yet having had a Taco Bell meal, my immediate thought was I could go to the supermarket and buy an Old El Paso taco kit and make a tastier meal myself. The Taco Bell I tried in Sydney was plain and gave me no reason to want to try it again. However, I've had it in the US several times and found it to be far superior to what I had in Sydney, and I'd be happy to have it again in the US.

The lesson the ABL could draw from Taco Bell is it is essential to adapt to consumer reaction quickly and work to have a firm understanding of what baseball fans want. Subsequently, the ABL should be adjusting its brand of baseball to the local market, and this is a graduated process, which as each season progresses will present the ABL with additional fan sentiment.

To the ABL's credit, it issued on its website detailed fan surveys at the end of the 2011/2012 season. I can't remember the last time I've seen a tier one or two sport in Australia issue a survey to fans seeking feedback of their product and performance. The other sports may well do this in some form, but in the decades I've followed sports in Australia I haven't come across one which covers as many facets as the ABL's. This is a mechanism which can assist with business strategic gap analysis and developing suitable tactical and operations plans. The ABL's survey gives me confidence they are willing to listen, learn, and implement.

Starbucks coffee had a dramatic rise and an even swifter rationalisation in Australia during the 2000s. As a multicultural country, Australia has very diverse taste for coffee, and its coffee culture has evolved over time to include European and Middle Eastern styles. Starbucks presented as a unique north-western American brand that appeared to be more like hot coffee–flavoured smoothies than Italian espresso. It gave consumers another choice and worked well enough to have eighty-four stores Australia-wide—yet this ambitious drive for expansion was its main undoing, as it tried to compete directly with a coffee shop culture which is often store-to-store unique. Standardisation of coffee in Australia is not especially conducive to the norm of the market because of the range of variation. Local company Gloria Jean's is making a go of franchised coffee and provides familiar varieties and snacks. It has experienced successes and failures, but in doing so has stabilised its market share.

Starbucks closed sixty-one of its eighty-four Australian stores in 2008, but this decision allowed the brand to operate as an American speciality, and with the benefit of hindsight this is probably how it should have aimed to trade all along.

For the purpose of strategic planning of sports, Starbucks offers a prime example of two deadly factors in Australia's market. The first was expanding before solidifying, as while it is possible to be initially profitable, it is sustained profits over a longer period of time which sorts out the novelty value success from the products that have captured the hearts and minds of consumers. The second is the art of knowing your market. Starbucks' higher quantity sizes were vastly excessive compared to the local market's definition of large cup. Also, there appeared to be a lack of effort by them to try to incorporate more of the local popular choices of coffee to their range. Subsequently, while attempting to assimilate local taste and interests may cause a brand to diversify from its traditional variants, adding localised choices creates a wider purchasing opportunity for the consumer, which helps keep customers in stores.

The ABL could apply Starbucks' Australian experience as points to note on a number of levels, but one that stands out for me is the way in which local culture can play such a pivotal role in achieving success or failure.

Baseball is the same game wherever it is played around the world, yet local brands of baseball culture make it unique internationally. Culture is the foundation of any civilisation and baseball games often present fans with unique game-day experiences, which can include war cries, team songs, club history, and local popular music. From season one, fans of ABL clubs across Australia quickly developed their own war cries and ABL culture continues to grow with each season, and this is an attribute of the game which helps give baseball in Australia its own brand.

The one aspect of the ABL I'd like to see enhanced, is the building up of the culture of the sport to ensure it looks and sounds as Australian as possible.

It's always pleasing to make new mates through baseball and by following the website BaseballdeWorld and adding discussion comments to postings I'm fortunate to know the managing editor American Eric Bynum.

Bynum, an English teacher in South Korea since 2009, has been a baseball fan for well over thirty years, having played, coached, and written about the game since he was a child. He went to South Korea in the hope of seeing baseball in other parts of the world. Through his website, Baseballde-World, he covers baseball all over the world. In doing so, he hopes to bring attention to the game on a worldwide level while helping advance the game in underdeveloped areas.

Bynum provided some excellent insights on what stands out for him in South Korea; in his e-mail to me dated March 17, 2012:

> Korean baseball culture is one of strict team spirit. It starts before the game as they file into the stadium to fill up their thunderstix with air. The fans in Korea root for a full nine innings regardless of the score. Always cheering, and never jeering the opposition, the fans chant, sing, and yell for their favourite team in synchronised form from start to finish without exception. They are fascinated with the game and hold on hard to their heroes wherever they play. They view the game with such passion that it's contagious.

With this in mind, the ABL has an opportunity to develop a culture unique to Australia. But it must be a collective effort, involving the fans, the ABL, and the league teams.

To achieve this goal it is important to be ever mindful of what is considered local and foreign, and how these factors influence the identity of the sport. There are two points within the ABL, which aren't consistent with Australia's sporting landscape, the first using the term "Will Call" at ticket booths. "Will Call" is not the term used for collecting pre-organised tickets in person, which is essentially what it means in North America. In Australia, if you're collecting tickets at the venue, there is a window at the ticket booth usually marked "Ticket Collection" or "Prepaid Tickets." To introduce a term people aren't familiar with locally is a misnomer and demonstrates a flaw in knowing the local market.

The second is the playing of the Australian National Anthem at every ABL game. This is again inconsistent with the rest of Australia's sporting landscape. Generally in Australia, the national anthem is only played for special events like grand finals. On one hand, I'm certainly in favour of greater nationalism in Australia, on the other, it's copying practices from the US. To some degree this creates a divide with people who are new to baseball, as they don't see it as being Australian to play the anthem before regular season games.

The ABL may wish to consider if it wants to blend more into the Australian sporting landscape or take a different approach which may be perceived as replicating baseball culture from the US.

Decoratively, the ABL can take more opportunities to assign an Australian identity to the sport. I've noticed red, white, and blue rosette and ribbon decorations appear at some ABL venues, which looks quite smart but is not Australian enough for me. The ABL could display more inflatable kangaroos in baseball playing attire and greater use of the Southern Cross to reinforce a visage that is Australian. These aren't by any means new design ideas as both images have been used as Team Australia logos at various times. Greater use of these would enable the ABL to capitalise in terms of giving the sport a greater local face.

The fact baseball is considered foreign to many local sports fans is part of the reason the ABL needs to somewhat overcompensate by offering a very Australian image.

I've attended NBL and ABL games with friends over the years and one attribute of both sports which seems to deter some people's interest, according to them, is baseball and basketball don't sound Australian enough. For example American ground announcers, on-field entertainers, radio and television commentators grate with some new spectators. For people who have always followed sports with an Australian voice behind a microphone, it's foreign to them.

Another issue which causes some people to be lukewarm about baseball is the fact they haven't played the sport and don't feel connected to it. Participation in any sport certainly contributes to a following, on the bright side, baseball is evolving in Australia and the more it is presented to people in the media, the better informed the general public becomes of Australia's capability in the sport. The ABL significantly complements these dynamics and provides a vehicle for the sport to attract new patronage and participation.

A massive potential breakthrough for baseball in Australia is the possibility of MLB opening a season in Australia, with Sydney mentioned as a possible host. MLB has played games in Sydney before, albeit back in 1914 when the New York Giants played the Chicago White Sox. Playing for the Giants was one of America's greatest all-round athletes, Jim Thorpe, a multiple Olympic gold medallist. While baseball may not have been a familiar sport in Australia then, Jim Thorpe was very well-known.

It has been suggested a revamped Sydney Cricket Ground (SCG) could possibly host an opening series. Not since the Sydney 2000 Olympic Games does baseball have a potentially bigger opportunity to win the hearts and minds of locals with a significant marquee event.

To put into perspective what a spectacle it could be, on August 7, 1999, the NFL brought the American Bowl to Sydney and put on a game featuring gridiron heavyweights Denver Broncos and San Diego Charges. It was played at the Olympic Stadium, and 73,811 spectators attended. This was a fantastic opportunity to see NFL-standard gridiron played on Australian soil and gave people around the world a sneak preview of the main Sydney Olympic venue.

While gridiron has a following in Australia, more people play baseball. We've achieved greater success in MLB than in the NFL, although we seem to be supplying the NFL with a few punters and making some progress with players in other positions too.

It's highly possible the SCG could achieve sell-out crowds hosting an MLB opening series and it would be an incredible publicity drive for the sport in Australia. An additional benefit is showcasing Sydney, which was nicely done during the American Bowl as they featured landmarks coming in and out of commercial breaks. Given the ABL All-Star Game and Championship Series has such international reach, Tourism Australia could benefit from a similar approach and if they got behind the ABL with such events.

As a growing sport, the ABL needs to be the smartest amongst its nearest competitors, the NBL and the A-League. Australia has hopefully awakened from its fanciful dream of hosting the Football World Cup Finals after an embarrassing waste of tens of millions of dollars with a failed bid—and a capital F for failure. If the public had been more aware other sports would lose some funding because of the bid, the idea would have received the negative attention it deserved and saved Australia some embarrassment.

Despite soccer's fumbling attempts to develop commendable strategic planning, it is able to fleece more than its fair share of local funding because every four years when the Football World Cup Finals come around, the A-League is seen as a vehicle which can assist Australia toward qualifying in World Cups by supporting domestic soccer. If soccer accepts it will never be Australia's number one sport, their planning would become a lot more realistic.

The A-League has considerable local resources at its disposal, vastly more extensive than the ABL's and this is why the ABL has to make every move or decision count.

The ABL has a much slimmer marketing budget compared to sports like the A-League; however it is possible for the ABL to carry out market research and development without swanky advertising agencies or expensive market research houses. The ABL could potentially engage university faculties and build a relationship whereby the students earn academic attainment for their projects, the ABL would benefit from their conclusions which could be used to assist with strategic market plans, control points, marketing management, and in reaching strategic goals and decisions. It could be particularly enticing for postgraduate students whose work could potentially end up in the hands of the ABL's or MLB's executive.

The ABL could become a leader among Australian sports in terms of involving universities with research and development, this may help highlight baseball as a sport for which university graduates could aim for and become actively involved with, ahead of the other sporting codes.

Internships in Australia aren't as common as in North America, as the Australian labour market is more inclined toward work experience placements of two to four weeks. Generally, there is an expectation in the Australian labour market that interning should have a paid job at the end of it for good performance, and with durations of months rather than weeks, interning doesn't heavily attract in Australia without the incentive of eventually attaining a paid job. This is why building a relationship with universities is of such value, because while the students may not receive a salary for their work they will be rewarded with the completion of their academic pursuit and develop a relationship with the sport.

The more volunteer duties of the ABL and aspects of research, development and marketing which can fall under an academic attainment umbrella, the greater capacity for the ABL to attract university students to the game. This could also involve sport/business management.

The ABL team Perth Heat has established a relationship with Edith Cowan University's faculty of business and law, and hopefully this will encourage each team to build a relationship with a local university. The ABL could potentially put forward some focus areas each season for projects to aim toward, which could assist in all the teams having some uniform areas of study. The ABL could also develop a relationship with a university itself as its functions may differ somewhat from those of the teams.

There are numerous university faculties which could assist baseball, including departments of history to help document the game in Australia, sociology with research and studying community relations and exercise and sports management.

The ABL is a macro vehicle for baseball in Australia and fans can certainly do their bit to support it by attending games, tuning in to televised games and buying merchandise. However enthusiasts can do much at a micro level, and whilst playing and supporting the game are very helpful contributions, the sport could benefit significantly from people actively campaigning for the ABL. In an age of social media, fans can do their bit to help make other people aware of the ABL by posting details of upcoming games, describing baseball plays they enjoy, and encouraging family, friends and colleagues to experience it.

The growth of baseball within Australia has many encouraging factors which can all contribute toward its local growth and sustainability. If Australia's involvement and contribution to the sport can be presented to North America through several mediums, its ability to prosper for the long-term could receive a significant boost.

CHAPTER 11
TAKING AUSTRALIAN BASEBALL ACROSS NORTH AMERICA

Australia is a place North Americans have an interest in; the number of American tourists who visit, and my own experiences there, confirm this. But it is larger-than-life Australian personalities like Paul Hogan as Crocodile Dundee and Steve Irwin, the energetic Crocodile Hunter, who have both proved to be big hits there.

It stands to reason that Australian MLB players with lively demeanours and plenty of skills on the baseball field could go a way to help depict an image and character of Australian baseball, which could help generate further interest in Aussie participation in the sport.

Relief pitcher Grant Balfour sometimes exhibits the temper of a Tasmanian devil when a pitch misses or he experiences a bit of bad luck with the bounce of a ball, yet his self-directed outbursts are the type of behaviour that can get a crowd excited and add a colourful mood to a moment. The fact Balfour is sometimes associated with the Tasmanian devil by the American press is a double dose of Australia, and his long career is not only a testament to his talent on the mound but he's also a living billboard of baseball from Australia. Each time he pitches, he gives fans and commentators calling games a reason to think and talk about the Land Down Under.

Pitcher Travis Blackley's renaissance 2012 season with the Oakland A's helped display his potential, and he attracted American media attention because he had taken a long road to get there. It is human nature, though, to enjoy a story in which a person overcomes numerous setbacks and then achieves when an opportunity is presented to them, which was consistent with Blackley earning a spot in the A's pitching rotation. Often when he made a start, commentators calling the game would talk a bit about Australia, which was amplified on the back of his successes.

Blackley's interest in heavy metal music and his tattoos and body piercings makes him standout, and being an Aussie certainly gives people many reasons to remember him.

The fact that he and Balfour have had an opportunity to play alongside each other on the A's combines to make them both highly active ambassadors for Aussie baseball—having multiple Australians on any team does a lot to perpetuate an Australian theme, which is often supported by many media interview questions about life back home.

Peter Moylan is yet another character, but it is his frequency of relief appearances on the mound which does plenty to promote Australia. Based on his career to date, he has appeared in eighty or more games per season three times. This presents home and visiting radio or television commentators an opportunity to mention Australia in nearly half the games of a regular season. Often when he is introduced by radio or television broadcasters, it is something like, "Moylan the Australian" or "Australian-born Peter Moylan coming into the game," and the mention of Australia gives millions of baseball fans a prompt to associate the game they enjoy with

Australia. Also, as he accumulates more seasons he becomes additionally familiar to home and away fans, and his ability to get outs and be successful gives supporters further reasons to take interest in him.

As most Australians who have played MLB are pitchers, having an Aussie appear in all 162 regular season games is something which will hopefully occur in due course, but everyday positional players have been infrequent, with Dave Nilsson as one who achieved it during his career.

The larger the stage, the greater the opportunity to associate Australia with baseball, and Nilsson appearing in the 1999 All-Star Game, Graeme Lloyd playing on two World Series winning teams in 1996 and 1998 and Grant Balfour appearing in the 2008 World Series were all mega opportunities to tell millions of people that baseball is played in Australia too…and feel free to visit anytime.

It was quite amazing to have so much happen in the late 1990s, yet there is still more to aim for, such as an Aussie in an All-Star game starting line-up or achieving Most Valuable Player season honours or during playoff or World Series play, just to name a few very substantial goals. All these hopes are multilayered as an Aussie player's success on the field is also a win for their country. I wonder how many American tourists have visited Australia because of an Aussie player on a team or participating in a sport they follow. Developing an interest in a foreign land can be stimulated by a person who hails from there and is admired for their skills and character. Actor Hugh Jackman has no doubt contributed toward a flow of tourists coming to Australia.

It's fine to have Australian baseball players as a vital part of the marketing drive, but more components are needed to achieve the fullest results. The Arts is one area where there is potential for enormous reach and the chance to attract people who may not follow baseball closely.

A quality Australian-themed baseball film could be a significant breakthrough locally and in North America, not to mention just about anywhere in the world. The movie *Moneyball* was a hit for many reasons with fans of baseball as well as people who have never followed the sport. One reason which stands out for me was the avant-garde approach of trying to achieve success with undervalued resources, which collectively contributed to positive outcomes because of effective usage. Baseball can therefore be considered as a metaphor for a significant message in terms of attaining high-performance outcomes by taking a different approach and appreciating how specific individual skills, which may not stand out as the typical attributes to achieve success, can all combine in a team environment and present exceptional results.

Films often convey multiple narrative implications which capture viewers at a deeper level. Therefore a baseball movie with a focus on the sport and other broader issues has enhanced capacity to capture interest. When it comes to any potential Australian baseball film, it is essential for the story to be able to cross the sports line and into the mainstream viewer domain. I am aware of several ideas for an Aussie-themed movie, but one which stands out for me is Peter Moylan's journey. From my experiences writing books, it seems there is a strong interest in true stories, particularly when it comes to sports genre, as there is a tendency for greater reader satisfaction knowing that what they have read actually happened to someone. Also, well-known sports books and films seem to be most often based on true-life events. With this in mind, a movie that follows some of Moylan's life and baseball career can work toward a higher probability of success because this is what the market prefers.

Moylan's story is unique for many reasons, including him being a rare case of a player having a second coming after years away from professional baseball, he's an Aussie, an energetic character, and he has lasted in MLB despite injury setbacks. While his story has similarities to the baseball film *The Rookie,* both have very different circumstances and I'm convinced each offers an inspiring and entertaining story.

I'm not the first person to mention the film potential of Moylan's story, and it might be a few years off because he is still actively playing MLB, but I'm satisfied this is the most suitable proposal for an Australian baseball film. There will probably be only one chance to make an Australian-themed movie, which is added incentive to make it a winner. Sports films made in Australia have a mixed track record with very few standouts, and so this is a bit more pressure for a baseball story to contend with, but it could make a success even sweeter.

The combination of taking America's national summer pastime and adding an Australian flavour would appear to be a happy marriage, as baseball is a very familiar subject for Americans and Australia is a country which seems to be of interest to many people there.

The American market is a special place to do business because there appear to be no limitations in terms of how far a popular product can go. It is common in the music industry to "have made it" by succeeding in the US. An Australian baseball film has an inside track on cracking one of the biggest markets in the world. An interesting example to consider is the Australian television soap opera *Neighbours,* which during the late 1980s and early 1990s was watched by more people in the United Kingdom than the entire population of Australia at the time. Australia's population back then was about nineteen million people.

With a 2010 population of about twenty-two million people, Australia has a growing market, but this is dwarfed by a US market of close to 300 million. If an Australian movie captured the attention of North Americans, it could flow into every baseball market in the world, and if the story had enough key events and layers to appeal to general viewers, its global reach could be close to a billion people. This without a doubt would be the biggest break for baseball in Australia.

If the movie could be constructed bilaterally by Hollywood and the Australian Film Industry, with filming in Australia and in the United States, its potential to attract funding would be enhanced, and this could also mean utilising some of the best production companies in the world.

A documentary about Australian baseball is long overdue and this could be the impetus to start taking Australia's participation in the sport to the screen. I'm sure Australia's governing body for baseball (the Australian Baseball Federation) would very much like to do this, but funding is an issue for many film and television projects in Australia, and often consortiums are needed to cover production cost.

There are many approaches to a documentary which could be utilised, but a work examining players and perhaps the era from the mid-1980s to the end of the 2000s would have enormous capability to capture the stories of Australia's baseball trailblazers who grew up and took to the sport in Australia and became Major Leaguers. Having Craig Shipley, Dave Nilsson, Graeme Lloyd, Grant Balfour, and Peter Moylan at centre, with many other Aussie Major Leaguers contributing, could be a wonderful package. It would be essential to examine their playing but also their experiences as Aussies abroad and their lives back home where their exploits in North America aren't as well-known.

An Aussie documentary which presents viewers with actual events in terms of gameplay footage and anecdotes could be highly engaging, and there are so many baseball fanatics in North America who would be interested in watching if such a documentary existed. Like a feature film, it would combine details fans may already know or be familiar with, yet the personal insights and the concentration on Australian participation would be new and informative for all fans. It would also be fantastic for Australia to have its own stories presented as two-dimensional points of reference, which would be enticing viewing for existing Australian enthusiasts of the sport and also offer people new to the sport proof of what Aussie players have achieved and why they may consider taking an interest in the game.

At present, there isn't a lot of Australian baseball printed literature out there, although Joe Clark's *A History of Australian Baseball: Time and Game* has certainly helped provide some momentum. There are many staunch baseball supporters in North America who enjoy reading books which cover the game from all over the world. This is why the more Aussie literature there is, the better chance that Australia's participation will become more widely known to Americans and a higher number of Australians.

Baseball-themed books are a genre in America which has a readership in the millions and Australia could attract more interest through this medium, with success in the US potentially doing a lot to ensure that the same books are on shelves in shops in Australia. It's no coincidence when *Moneyball* was featured in Australian cinemas, Australian bookstores carried the book version of the story. When it comes to baseball in Australia, retailers are more likely to follow positive US sales experience, which is due in part to the still-emerging profile of the sport in Australia.

Literature is a place where so much Australian baseball history and stories can be recorded. Films, books, and television with an Australian baseball theme are all very helpful in building up the culture of the sport locally and also offering Americans and people worldwide with an Aussie baseball experience.

My goal with my own baseball-themed books has always been to try to maintain the attention of not only those interested in the game but also general readers, which is why my narratives include events that occur around the sport, not just what takes place on the field.

The ABL could play a central role in taking Australian baseball across North America by becoming a highly desired winter league to play in, and there are several key factors which could fuel interest. To begin with, the standard of play in the ABL includes players with Major League experience, and this offers all players the opportunity to test their skills against those who have played at higher levels than them, or it presents an opportunity to receive game time to enhance the development of new skills and gain further experience.

For Americans, playing in the ABL doesn't present overt language barriers, and culturally Australia has many similarities. Notwithstanding this, there are numerous players who have participated in the ABL who are from all over the world and don't speak English as a first language so the league certainly has an international flavour—yet the game is the common language which unites all.

The previous ABL was played at a time when some of the communications modes of today were just coming into their infancy. Back in the late 1980s and into the 1990s, American import players could contact family or friends in the US with either post mail or an expensive long-distance phone call; this meant many of their achievements in the ABL or experiences in Australia had limited reach. These days, the world is a lot closer and social media is instantaneous. Subsequently, American players are almost like delegates for Australia because every e-mail or posting causes family, friends, and other players to associate Australia with each communication they receive.

There is a positive tendency by people to become moved to try something because someone they know or a family member has experienced it. As a result of Americans participating in the ABL, they may contribute toward a teammate wanting to play in the league or family and friends choosing to holiday in Australia.

The flashiest television commercial, prettiest model, catchiest jingle and most striking billboard all pale in comparison to the trust people take from someone they respect.

In time, it may be possible for the ABL to increase its international coverage to an extent where weekly games are televised in North America. The ABL has made progress with television coverage during each of its first two seasons.

Providing Australian viewers with weekly televised games would contribute toward local audience growth, yet if the league became known among American fans, their viewer patronage could contribute toward significant ratings. There are supporters of the game who would be happy to watch baseball all year round, and the ABL could be one means to help them do so. Asia also presents an enormous potential viewership.

A tried-and-proven method of taking Australian baseball across America is the continuous and hopefully increasing flow of Australians participating in college and professional baseball in America. These players will always be Aussie baseball ambassadors and each time they play in a town or city, they give local people a reason to think about Australia.

If Australia can continually expand its baseball visibility on a micro and macro level in North America, the association of the sport to Australia could become deeper, leading to additional investment in the ABL and more programs supporting baseball development, further boosting Australia as a country of interest for Americans and a desired place to visit.

CHAPTER 12
POSTSCRIPT

It has been an honour to be interviewed and mentioned by various Baseball News services, and a particularly special opportunity was to assist Rory Costello from the Society for American Baseball Research (SABR) in 2011 and 2012 regarding Australian Major Leaguers.

The SABR documents history, statistics, and biographies and carries out several other baseball-related services. Germans are known for their meticulous record-keeping, but Americans and the SABR certainly set an impressive standard.

For many sports in Australia, it's difficult to find online archived records of past seasons' game results, game-day articles, and individual statistics for players (past and present) which are continually updated. Even Australia's top tier sports don't appear to provide much in the way of archived online records. On MLB.com, their archive goes back years and I've been able to extract information from games close to a decade old, and the service Baseball-Reference.com (which SABR contributes to) is a wealth of information on past and current professional players. To be able to assist a SABR project was certainly a buzz for me.

Rory Costello is a long-time member of SABR, and he lives in Brooklyn, New York, with his wife Noriko and four-year-old son Kai. In the late 1990s, he thought about writing for one of the SABR annuals and cast about for a topic which hadn't been previously unearthed. He remembered going on family vacations to the US Virgin Islands as a boy, and when he collected baseball cards, a number of players had gone from there to the Majors.

Several years later, the SABR Bio Project website—an effort to gather short biographies of every man who has played in the Majors—came into being.

Over time, Costello's effort which began with the Virgin Islanders branched out into a broader effort to celebrate the game's international dimension. He has now written about players from nearly twenty countries, including Australia.

Costello discovered blog postings I wrote regarding Dave Nilsson and Craig Shipley and contacted me. This came as a very pleasant surprise and I was more than happy to assist him. The players he focused on were Shipley, Nilsson, Graeme Lloyd, and Trent Durrington. He cited me in all of these players' biographies and I was quoted in Nilsson's biography, which was a wonderful honour.

Records of the previous ABL, such as players' statistics aren't easily attainable and I was able to provide Costello with statistics and other information.

Upon completing his project, I asked him for details of aspects he found rewarding, and he told me:

> The research in itself is rewarding. It's great fun to see different nations through the prism of baseball and see how each has influenced the other. In addition to world history, finding out more about the men who have played the game—and whenever possible, working directly with them—has also made this hobby enjoyable. With

> particular regard to Australia, it was intriguing to find out about the nation's club scene. The influence of several men in particular is notable: Barry Shipley (father of Craig Shipley, the first Aussie born and trained Major Leaguer), Dick Shirt (who played professionally in the US as far back as 1967), and Kevin Greatrex (who also played US pro ball in '67 and scouted Nilsson).

I found all of Costello's short biographies to be informative and his use of an active voice at times in the body of these works contributed toward making them as two-dimensional as possible and engaging reading.

It is my hope more and more of Australia's baseball history will be recorded, and I'm very fortunate the tenure of my interest has occurred at a time where so much has happened, yet I look forward to much more.

To this day, I'm perplexed as to why baseball's cousin softball was dropped as a women's event at the Summer Olympic Games. When it comes to the spirit of the Olympics, softball seemed to tick so many boxes with the Olympics as the apex of their game, most players having amateur status, a lack of fully professional leagues worldwide, and it is played competitively by many countries, including Australia. Yet it was decided to not continue with it at the Olympics, which I feel was a mistake. Softball deserves another hit, and it is sad a generation of players won't be able to participate in the sport at the Olympic level. With a bit of luck, softball will hopefully return to the Olympics by 2020.

Men's baseball also lost its place in the Olympics after Beijing 2008, and for it to return, it could benefit by implementing some changes to its previous structures. I feel women's baseball—more than men's—has a rightful place at the

Olympics (it's never previously been a women's medal sport) given that many of the world's most elite female players are amateurs, and the ones who earn some income playing do so in leagues and competitions where the earnings go toward covering living expenses with perhaps a small amount left over. Therefore the Olympics would certainly be the ultimate goal for women playing the game and I'm in favour of sports where a gold medal is the highest achievement as this is more in keeping with the fundamentals of Olympic status sports.

Men's baseball had a period of Olympic status from 1992–2008, with 1992 and 1996 permitting amateur participants only and 2000, 2004, and 2008 allowing professional players. Men's baseball never had true Dream Teams like basketball, which was in part due to the Olympic schedule clashing with professional leagues like MLB, NPB, the KBO, and the CPBL. Winning a MLB World Series is the sport's greatest prize, and while a gold medal is a tremendous achievement, Olympic status isn't so deeply steeped in the sport.

However, men's baseball could become more appealing for Olympic competition if it adopted a model similar to Olympic football (soccer). Specifically, having a team of players under twenty-three years of age with four over aged players allowed on the team; two could be positional players, and two could be pitchers. All players can be professionals, but there would be a greater focus on emerging talent under this model. At the Olympic level, there is merit in considering more professional sports such as tennis and basketball in this light too, as it is one way to find ground between amateur and professional players, and it is more consistent with the traditional ethos of the Olympics.

I'm certainly not the first person to hypothesize—as per the suggestions I've made—softball and baseball's return to

Olympic competition, yet having these sports at the Olympics is enriching. All these sports are played on several continents and by millions of people, so any arguments to assert they are niche sports is erroneous.

Olympic softball and baseball would be helpful for both sports in Australia as it could help each gain more local funding by reclaiming Olympic status. The Australian government provided additional finances toward these sports, most notably for the Sydney 2000 Olympic Games. There is a tendency by governments in Australia to become more fund-friendly toward sports where there is reasonable potential for a medal, and both softball and baseball are games Australia has previously won Olympic medals in.

One aspect of baseball in Australia which has caught my attention recently is second- and third-generation baseball players with professional stock in the family. When Phil Dale's son Ryan signed with the Kansas City Royals in 2012, it became clear baseball is building a deeper place for itself in the sporting landscape. Phil played minor league baseball and in the previous ABL and now Ryan will pursue his own professional career.

The ABL's word for the present and future is "sustainability," and with this at the centre of planning and management decisions, its growth and longevity are more and more possible.

Baseball is a game which can make strangers into friends, and this can occur as a player, spectator, or an enthusiast of the sport. The fact a person might be wearing my favourite team's cap is a reason to say "Hello" or cheer on the team, or if they're sitting next to me in a grandstand at a game, the play on the field can be a reason to engage in conversation and share stories and perspectives.

I've been so fortunate to see many great games and be a guest of Major League clubs, but the most valuable personal riches for me are the friends I've made and the memories we share, thanks to the sport bringing us together.

Baseball is a compass in my life.

CPSIA information can be obtained at www.ICGtesting.com
Printed in the USA
LVOW04s1943090615

441778LV00035B/1419/P